IMAGES
of America

ROCKY RIVER

OHIO

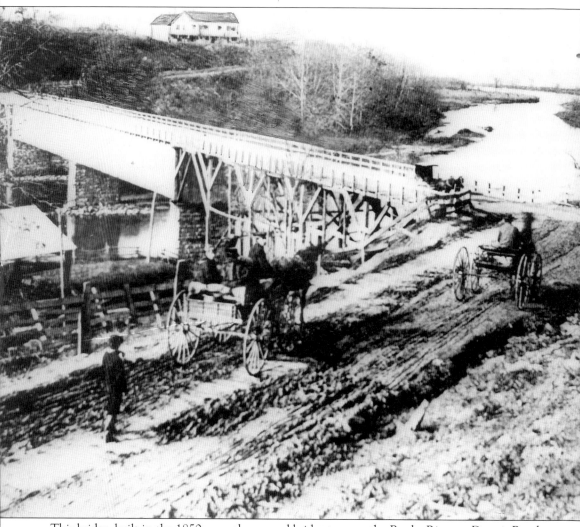

This bridge, built in the 1850s, was the second bridge to span the Rocky River at Detroit Road. The photograph was taken from the Lakewood side of the river. The large white building on the opposite bank is the Silverthorne Tavern. (Photograph Courtesy of Cleveland Press Archives at Cleveland State University.)

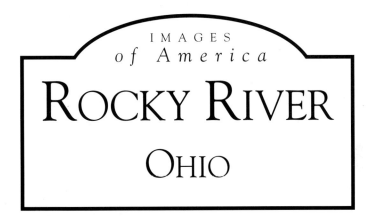

IMAGES
of America

ROCKY RIVER

OHIO

Carol Lestock

ARCADIA

Published by Arcadia Publishing,
an imprint of Tempus Publishing, Inc.
3047 N. Lincoln Ave., Suite 410
Chicago, IL 60657

Printed in Great Britain.

Library of Congress Catalog Card Number: 2002106604

For all general information contact Arcadia Publishing at:
Telephone 843-853-2070
Fax 843-853-0044
E-Mail sales@arcadiapublishing.com

For customer service and orders:
Toll-Free 1-888-313-2665

Visit us on the internet at http://www.arcadiapublishing.com

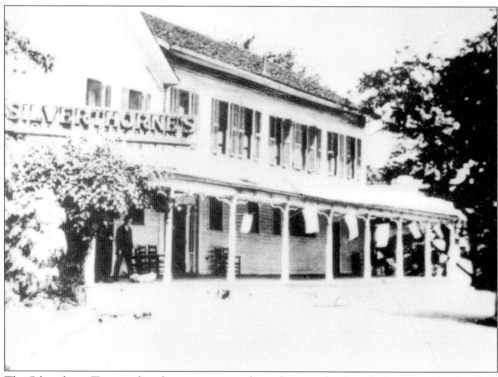

The Silverthorn Tavern played an important role in the growth of Rocky River. In the first half of the 19th century, travel through northern Ohio was by foot, horseback, or wagon. Taverns served as resting places and information centers where travelers exchanged news. Local people living some distance from each other would meet here to talk and drink. (Photograph Courtesy of Dugan's Barbershop.)

CONTENTS

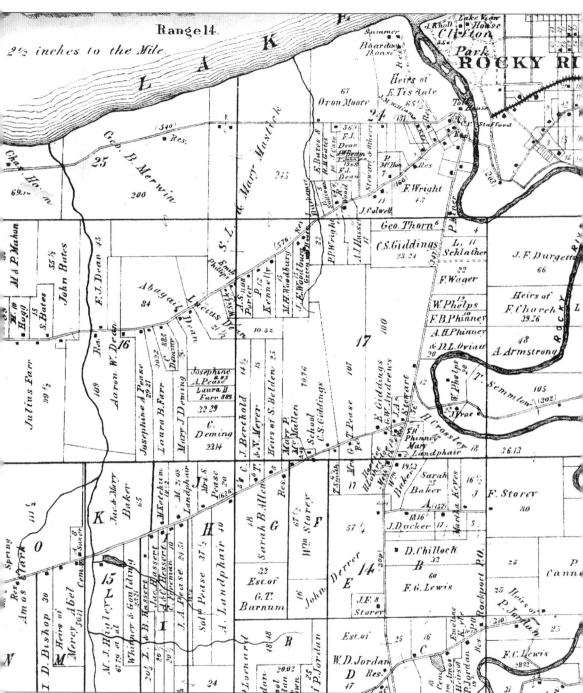

Township 7, Range 14 encompassed present-day Fairview Park, Lakewood, Rocky River, and the West Park neighborhood of Cleveland. In 1807, a group of businessmen purchased 21 square miles from the Connecticut Land Company and formed the township. Twelve years later, in 1819, the inhabitants of the area petitioned the county commissioners to name the township Rockport. The map above approximately encompasses that part of Rockport Township that included Rocky River as it is today.

INTRODUCTION

This book will attempt to introduce the reader to the history of Rocky River, Ohio, through photographs, maps and etchings. It is by no means a complete history, but rather a collection of various moments from the early days of the city, a visual history, a tour guide of the past.

Rocky River is home. Families stay there generation after generation and many people who have left Rocky River return. However, the majority of Riverites know very little about the history of their home. Very few physical reminders from the distant past exist, other than old documents, photographs, and memories of surviving older citizens. I hope this collection of photographs will help fill the void that progress has left behind.

I first got the idea to do this book when my Uncle Jack showed me old postcards of Rocky River from the early 1900s. I was fascinated to see a very different town superimposed on places that I know well. In most of the photographs natural landmarks, such as the river and the lake, were the only clues as to where the pictures were taken. Other photographs included structures that I remembered from my own youth, but now no longer exist. These images reminded me of the many conversations I had with my mother about what used to be where. She told me about a big farm off of Wooster Road, a sand pit behind her house on Rockland Avenue, where carnivals were held, a tennis court on a beach, and more. I began to wonder about the history of the place I call home. It was at this point that I realized that I wanted an album for myself that contained a visual history of Rocky River.

An historical photo album of Rocky River would not be complete without a few words about its early, pre-photographic history. One of the first written references to Rocky River concerns a 1764 expedition of a British officer, Colonel Bradstreet. He had traveled from Fort Niagara, New York, to Detroit, Michigan, in order to bring supplies to British troops stationed there and to replace some troops at Mackinaw, where there had been an Indian uprising in 1763. On Bradstreet's return trip along Lake Erie, he and his remaining troops camped at what is now known as Bradstreet's Landing in Rocky River. During the night a storm arose, and Bradstreet's company lost many of its boats and equipment. In what now is known as Bradstreet's Disaster, provisions were lost in the storm and there were not enough boats left to carry all Bradstreet's men back to Niagara.

The next mention of the area is in early histories of Cuyahoga County. The story of our town begins in 1805 when Gideon Granger, a Connecticut landowner, first explored the area at the mouth of the Rocky River. He envisioned a great city there that would overtake Cleveland and become a major port on the Great Lakes. While Granger's dream never came true, Rockport Township was formed in the area in 1807. Cleveland grew into a great industrial city while Rockport Township developed farms and fruit orchards on densely forested and somewhat swampy land. Eventually, small communities grew up within the township—East Rockport, or Lakewood, on the east side of the river and Rocky River on the west side.

As Cleveland's industry and pollution increased, more and more Clevelanders sought to escape the city on holidays and weekends. The area at the mouth of the Rocky River became a resort and recreation area. Towards the end of the 19th century, the arrival of electric streetcar service from Cleveland made it possible for Clevelanders to move out to Lakewood and Rocky River and continue to work in the city.

Rocky River was incorporated as a village, separate from Rockport, in 1903. As the city approaches its centennial, now is an appropriate time to look back on its past.

The names of places, streets and businesses change over time. For instance, Detroit Road was once North Ridge. The eastern end of Lake Road was Blount Street, and Wooster Road was Mastick Road for a time. The tavern on the location of the Westlake Hotel was known over the years as Wright's Tavern, Silverthorn Tavern (sometimes spelled Silverthorne), Patchen House, and Rocky River House. When explaining photographs I have tried to use the name in effect at the time the photograph was taken, with further detail if necessary.

One

THE EARLIEST YEARS

The territory of northeast Ohio, known as the Western Reserve, was originally claimed by the state of Connecticut. Many who visited it at the beginning of the 19th century were looking to purchase land from Connecticut either for their own purposes or as an investment. One such man was Judson Canfield who, with a group of investors, purchased the territory that today consists of Lakewood, Rocky River, Fairview Park, and the Cleveland neighborhood of West Park. The area was officially known as Township 7, Range 14.

Gideon Granger first visited the area around the mouth of the Rocky River in 1805. In 1809, Granger purchased part of the township land from the Connecticut investors. His purchase included roughly 20% of present-day Rocky River, bounded on the north by the lake, on the west by Wagar Road, on the south along the line of Shoreland Avenue, and on the east across the river to Clifton Park. He divided his land into lots and sold them at a land auction. Granger immodestly planned to call the new town Granger City. However, as Cleveland continued to grow there was less interest in the area around the Rocky River and the plan for Granger City never materialized.

Rockport Township did grow, albeit more slowly than Gideon Granger envisioned. The township was known for its farms and orchards. As Cleveland became more and more industrialized, the area around the Rocky River became a recreation destination for the inhabitants of the growing city.

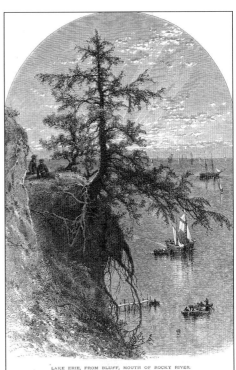

LAKE ERIE, FROM BLUFF, MOUTH OF ROCKY RIVER.

This etching is from *Picturesque America*, a two-volume history of the United States written by various travelers and edited by William Cullen Bryant. It was published in 1872 by D.C. Appleton.

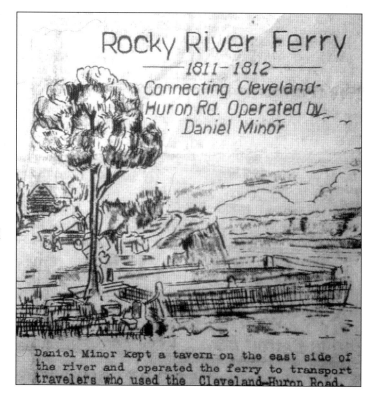

The earliest settler in the area was Philo Taylor, who came with his family from New York in the spring of 1808. He settled on the eastern side of the Rocky River near the mouth. Taylor and family lived there about a year before moving to Dover, just west of Rockport. The first resident west of the river was Datus Kelley, who in 1810 purchased the tract of land that was west of Wagar Road, between Detroit Road and Avalon. Kelley put up a sawmill on his land at Detroit and Elmwood. Kelley's brother-in-law, Chester Dean, moved to the area in 1811. Dean was to settle here permanently while Kelley moved out to what eventually became Kelley's Island. This etching shows a typical settler and family traveling to the Western Reserve. (Photograph Courtesy of Lakewood Historical Society.)

Daniel Miner moved to the Philo Taylor cabin in 1809. He started a ferry operation on the Rocky River, as the only way to cross the river at that time was by fording it. Miner has the dubious honor of being the first person indicted in the Court of Cuyahoga County. He was charged for illegally selling a gill (4 ounces) of whiskey and operating a ferry without a license. He then acquired licenses for both a ferry service and tavern on the eastern side of the river, as well as a saw mill. Miner died in 1813. (Photograph Courtesy of Lakewood Historical Society.)

Rocky River Ferry
—— 1811–1812 ——
Connecting Cleveland-Huron Rd. Operated by Daniel Minor

Daniel Minor kept a tavern on the east side of the river and operated the ferry to transport travelers who used the Cleveland-Huron Road.

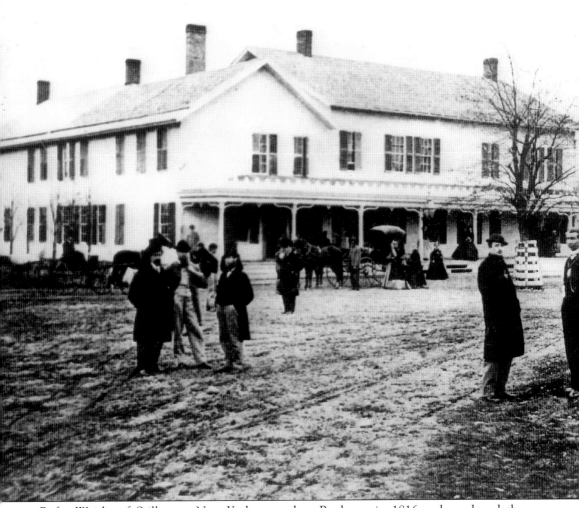

Rufus Wright of Stillwater, New York, moved to Rockport in 1816 and purchased three quarters of an acre from Gideon Granger. He built the Wright Tavern on the west side of the Rocky River. The tavern and land were located around the current site of the Westlake Hotel. Built before the first bridge over the Rocky River, early travelers from the east could reach the tavern by river ferry or ford. It was in the Wright Tavern where early settlers of the area met to discuss business and catch up on local news. In 1819, after petitioning the County Commissioners to give the name Rockport to Township 7 Range 14, the men of the area elected officers and held town meetings here. An early accomplishment of the town officers was the construction of the first bridge over the Rocky River, completed in 1821. Those participating in the first town meeting were: Rufus Wright, Ashahel Porter, Henry Canfield, Samuel Dean, Chester Dean, Dyer Nichols, Daniel Bardin, John Kidney, John Pitts, John James, Charles Miles, Erastus Johnson, Josephus Sizer, Datus Kelley, James Nicholson, Benjamin Robinson, and Henry Alger. (Photograph Courtesy of Cleveland Press Archives at Cleveland State University.)

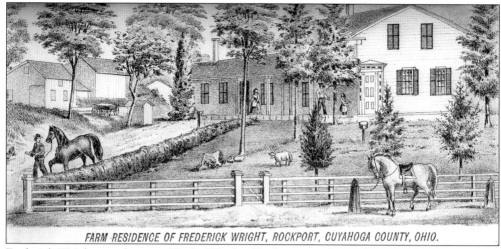

FARM RESIDENCE OF FREDERICK WRIGHT, ROCKPORT, CUYAHOGA COUNTY, OHIO.

Frederick Wright was the son of Rufus Wright. His house was located at Detroit Road between where Wright Avenue and Prospect Avenue are today. For many years the Wright family ran the post office, which was located at the Wright Tavern from 1834 until 1852. Rufus and his three sons all served as postmasters. It is fitting, then, that the previous Rocky River Post Office was located on Wright Avenue. (Graphic Courtesy of Cleveland State University Special Collections.)

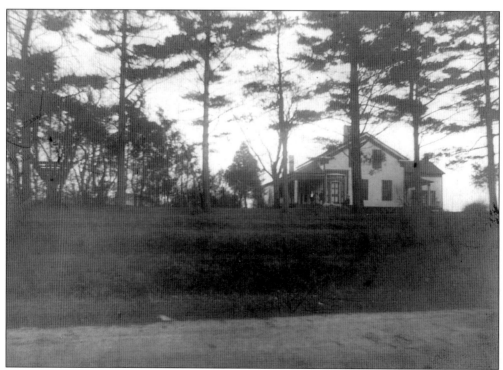

This photograph shows the Wright homestead in 1902. Frederick Wright raised apples, pears, cherries, and grapes on his 45 acres.

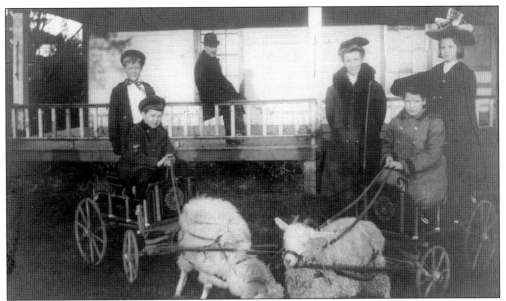

Relatives in for a Sunday visit from Cleveland are shown in this photograph taken in front of the Wright homestead. Larry and Pauline Strimple sit in wagons harnessed with goats. Behind them, from left to right, are Everett Sloat (behind Larry), J.L. Strimple (on the porch), Gertrude Arnold (standing), and Mildred Sloat (on the wagon behind Pauline).

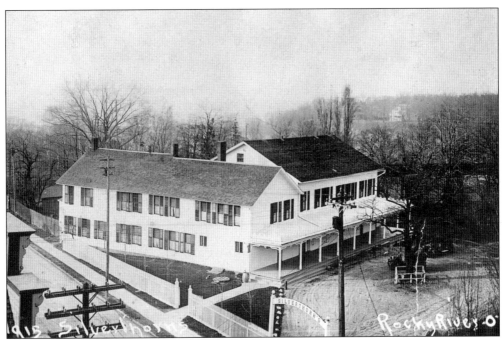

The Wright family sold the tavern to Jacob Silverthorn in 1853. He ran it until 1876, when he sold it to H. Patchen. For a time, the tavern was known both as the Patchen House and the Rocky River House. Several years later, Silverthorn bought the tavern back from Patchen and the establishment was once again known as Silverthorn Tavern until it was torn down circa 1920. (Photograph Courtesy of Rocky River Historical Society.)

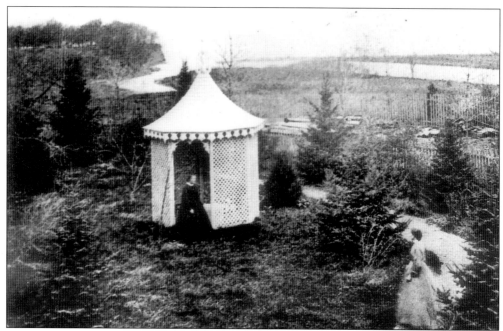

This photograph, circa 1865, was taken behind the Silverthorn Tavern. The road up from the bridge ran in back of the tavern. The tollhouse for the bridge can be seen at right. The island at the mouth of the Rocky River can be seen in the background. (Photograph Courtesy of the Cleveland Press Archives at Cleveland State University.)

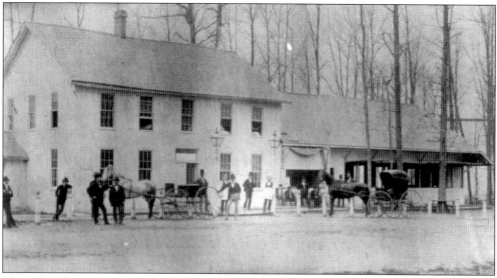

The Silverthorn Tavern had several counterparts on the eastern side of the Rocky River. According to the 1852 map of Rockport, Lake View House was located in Clifton Park. The name Rocky River originally referred to the area in Rockport on both the east and west side of the river. Early Clevelanders, according to an 1879 History of Cuyahoga County, came to Rocky River "in large numbers, to enjoy the beauties of nature and to rejoice in the invigorating breezes which are wafted landward over the billowy bosom of Lake Erie." (Photograph Courtesy of Lakewood Historical Society.)

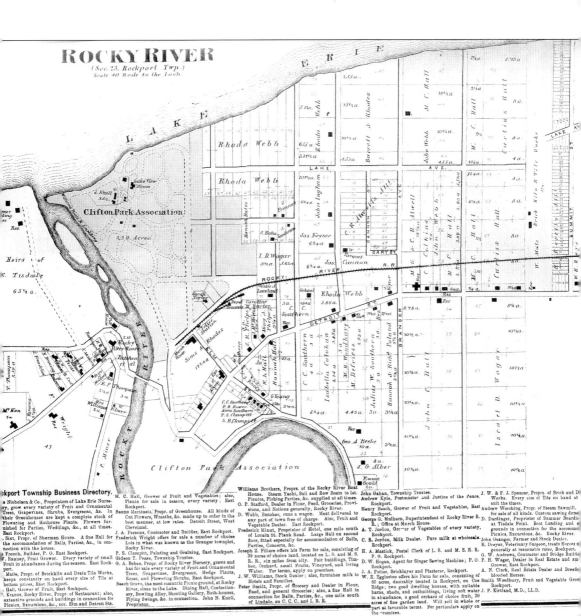

ROCKY RIVER

(Sec. 23. Rockport Twp.)
Scale 40 Rods to the Inch

...kport Township Business Directory.

...s Nicholson & Co., Proprietors of Lake Erie Nursery, grow every variety of Fruit and Ornamental Trees, Grapevines, Shrubs, Evergreens, &c. In their Greenhouses are kept a complete stock of Flowering and Hothouse Plants. Flowers furnished for Parties, Weddings, &c., at all times. East Rockport.

... Sixt, Propr. of Sherman House. A fine Hall for the accommodation of Balls, Parties, &c., in connection with the house.

... French, Builder, P. O. East Rockport.

... Ranney, Fruit Grower. Every variety of small Fruit in abundance during the season. East Rockport.

... Maile, Propr. of Brickkiln and Drain Tile Works, keeps constantly on hand every size of Tile at bottom prices, East Rockport.

... Hall, Grower of Fruit, East Rockport.

... Krauss, Rocky River, Propr. of Restaurant; also, extensive grounds and buildings in connection for Picnics, Excursions, &c., cor. Elm and Detroit Sts.

M. C. Hall, Grower of Fruit and Vegetables; also, Plants for sale in season, every variety; East Rockport.

Benno Martinetz, Propr. of Greenhouse. All kinds of Cut Flowers, Wreaths, &c. made up to order in the best manner, at low rates. Detroit Street, West Cleveland.

J. A. Parsons, Contractor and Builder, East Rockport.

Frederick Wright offers for sale a number of choice Lots in what was known as the Granger townplot, Rocky River.

P. S. Clampitt, Painting and Graining, East Rockport.

Gideon T. Pease, Township Trustee.

G. A. Bebee, Propr. of Rocky River Nursery, grows and has for sale every variety of Fruit and Ornamental Trees, Grapevines, Evergreens, Hedge Plants, Roses, and Flowering Shrubs, East Rockport.

Beech Grove, the most romantic Picnic ground, at Rocky River, close to the lake. Dining Hall, Confectionery, Bowling Alley, Shooting Gallery, Bath-houses, Flying Swings, &c. in connection. John N. Knoll, Proprietor.

Williams Brothers, Proprs. of the Rocky River Boat House. Steam Yacht, Sail and Row Boats to let. Picnics, Fishing Parties, &c. supplied at all times.

O. P. Stafford, Dealer in Flour, Feed, Groceries, Provisions, and Notions generally, Rocky River.

D. Webb, Butcher, runs a wagon. Meat delivered to any part of town free of charge. Also, Fruit and Vegetable Dealer. East Rockport.

Frederick Minut, Proprietor of Hotel, one mile south of Lorain St. Plank Road. Large Hall on second floor, fitted especially for accommodation of Balls, Parties, Concerts, &c.

Joseph Z. Filiere offers his Farm for sale, consisting of 39 acres of choice land, located on L. S. and M. S. R. R., six miles from city. Fair buildings, Timber, Orchard, small Fruits, Vineyard, and living Water. For terms, apply on premises.

J. W. Williams, Stock Dealer; also, furnishes milk to Hotels and Families.

Peter Smidt, Propr. of Grocery and Dealer in Flour, Feed, and general Groceries; also, a fine Hall in connection for Balls, Parties, &c., one mile south of Lindale, on C. C. C. and I. R. R.

John Gahan, Township Trustee.

Andrew Kyle, Postmaster and Justice of the Peace, Rockport.

Henry Beach, Grower of Fruit and Vegetables, East Rockport.

George G. Mulhern, Superintendent of Rocky River R. R.; Office at March House.

A. T. Jordon, Grower of Vegetables of every variety, Rockport.

C. R. Jordon, Milk Dealer. Pure milk at wholesale. Rockport.

H. A. Mastick, Postal Clerk of L. S. and M. S. R. R. P. O. Rockport.

D. W. Hogan, Agent for Singer Sewing Machine; P. O. Rockport.

J. A. Potter, Bricklayer and Plasterer, Rockport.

W. E. Eggleston offers his Farm for sale, consisting of 60 acres, desirably located in Rockport, on Coe Ridge; two good dwelling houses, with suitable barns, sheds, and outbuildings, living soft water in abundance, a good orchard of choice fruit, 30 acres of fine garden land. Will sell in whole or part at favorable terms. For particulars apply on the premises.

J. W. & F. J. Spencer, Proprs. of Brick and D... Works. Every size of Tile on hand at suit the times.

Andrew Worshing, Propr. of Steam Sawmill. for sale of all kinds. Custom sawing done

D. Dardinger, Proprietor of Summer Boardin... at Tisdale Point. Boat Landing and ... grounds in connection for the accommo... Picnics, Excursions, &c. Rocky River.

John Granger, Farmer and Stock Dealer.

H. Dreyer, Veterinary Surgeon, treats Horses a... generally at reasonable rates, Rockport.

G. W. Andrews, Contractor and Bridge Builde...

F. H. Wager, Dealer in Real Estate and an... Grower, East Rockport.

A. N. Clark, Real Estate Dealer and Breede... blooded Horses.

Smith Woodbury, Fruit and Vegetable Grow... Rockport.

J. P. Kirtland, M.D., LL.D.

This map from an 1874 atlas of Cuyahoga County appears to be a precursor of today's Yellow Pages. Because the map's emphasis seems to be business only, the western portion of Rocky River is not included. That area consisted primarily of farms. (Graphic Courtesy of Cleveland State University Special Collections.)

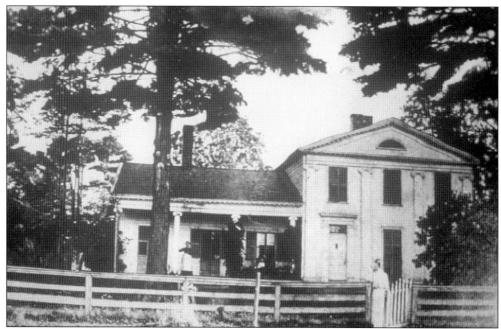

In 1834, Datus Kelley sold his farm and along with his brother moved to an island in Lake Erie, now known as Kelley's Island. He sold part of his land to Reuben Wood, a Cleveland lawyer. Wood built his home on the southwest corner of Avalon Drive and Wagar Road. He became a state legislator and was elected governor of Ohio in 1850. (Photograph Courtesy of Lakewood Historical Society.)

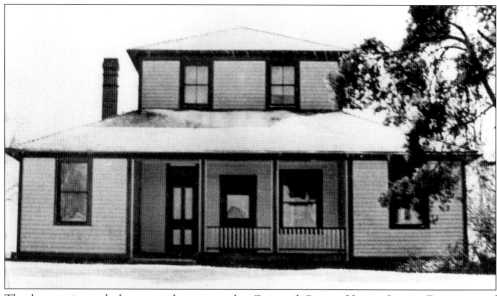

The house pictured above was known as the Cup and Saucer House. Lucius Dean, son of Chester and Lucy Dean, built the house in 1853. The first floor measured 40-by-40 feet, the second measured 20-by-20 feet. The house was torn down in 1963, despite the fact that the house was over a hundred years old, in order to make way for the Oxford Court apartments that grace Detroit Road today. (Photograph Courtesy of Rocky River Public Library.)

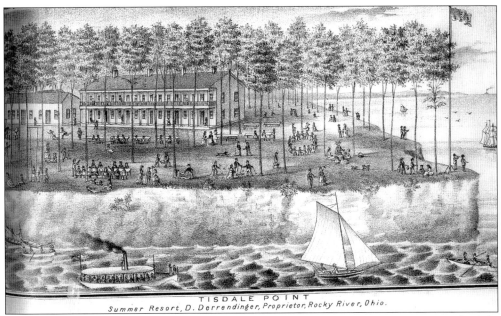

TISDALE POINT
Summer Resort, D. Derrendinger, Proprietor, Rocky River, Ohio.

The 1874 atlas locates this resort at the point on the west side of the Rocky River. It was built by Erastus Tisdale, an early settler to the Cleveland area. An advertisement in the atlas says the following about the resort: "D. Dardinger, Proprietor of Summer Boarding House at Tisdale Point. Boat Landing and extensive grounds in connection for the accommodation of Picnics, Excursions, &c. Rocky River." (Graphic Courtesy of Cleveland State University Special Collections.)

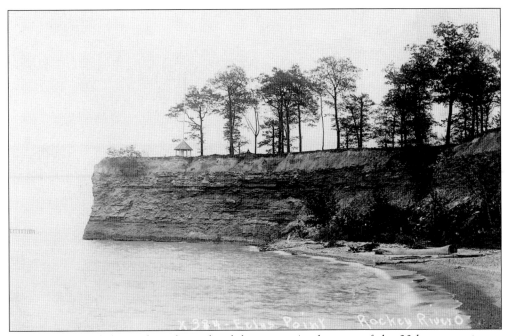

This old postcard shows the other side of the point. At the turn of the 20th century it was known as Ells Point, after the Ells family who lived on the property at that time.

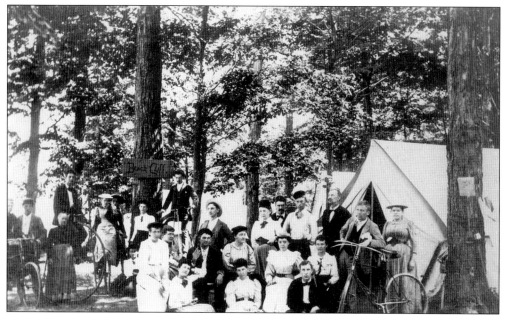

This photograph is identified as "Summer Camp" and was taken around 1895. The sign in the background says Beach Cliff, which refers to the area along the lake north of Lake Road. In 1888, Clifford Beach, businessman and congressman, purchased 427 acres along the lakeshore, including Reuben Wood's property. Beach's land was later sold for development and the area was called Beach Cliff in his honor. (Photograph Courtesy of Rocky River Public Library.)

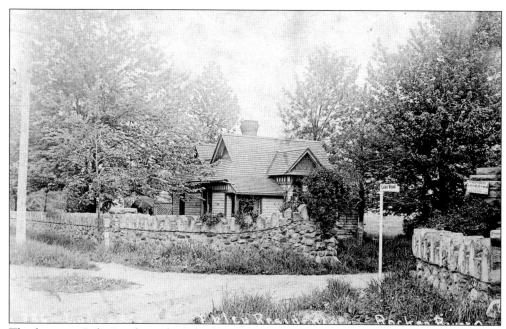

This house on Lake Road was the Erley home. Erley was the caretaker of the Beach estate. Parts of the stone wall, seen above, still stand today across from Bearden's Restaurant on Lake Road. The stone gateposts that stand today on the corners of Detroit Road and Erie marked another entrance to the Beach estate.

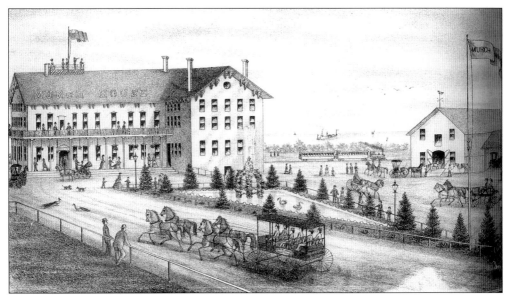

The Cliff House was built in 1863 on the land belonging to Daniel Miner's heirs, near Riverside and Edanola Streets in present-day Lakewood. It was a competitor of the Wright/Silverthorn Tavern. Both establishments were located at old ferry landings, which linked the east-west trail (Detroit Road) across northern Ohio. In 1873, Cliff House was re-named Murch House. (Graphic Courtesy of Cleveland State University Special Collections.)

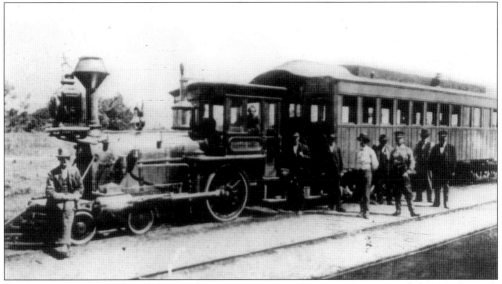

The Rocky River Railroad operated between 1869 and 1881. The start of the single-track railroad was at West 58th Street in Cleveland. The terminus was the Cliff House, making the railroad 6 miles in length. The railroad was popularly known as the "Dummy" Railroad. Dummy was a term used for small, quiet locomotives that ran on short railroads. During the summer months, the cars were full of passengers on their way to the beaches and parks at the mouth of the Rocky River. Because there were very few riders in the wintertime, the Rocky River Railroad did not last. The line was sold in 1881 to the Nickel Plate Railroad. (Photograph Courtesy of Lakewood Historical Society.)

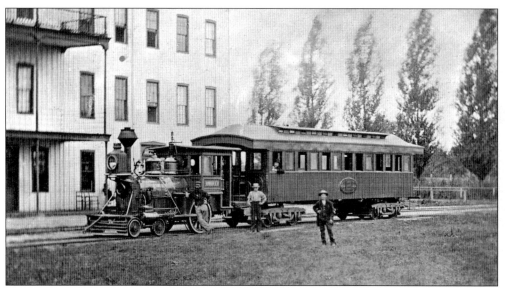

This photo shows the Dummy Railroad and crew ready for a run. The train is standing in front of the Murch House. The ticket office for the line was located on the first floor. (Photograph Courtesy of Rocky River Public Library.)

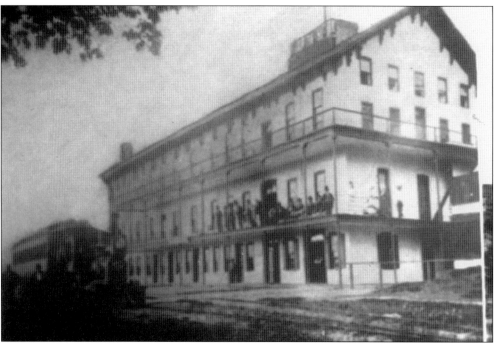

The Murch House had a bar on the first floor, a dining room on the second and a third-floor ballroom. The porch along the second story gave visitors a view of the river mouth and Lake Erie. (Photograph Courtesy of Lakewood Historical Society.)

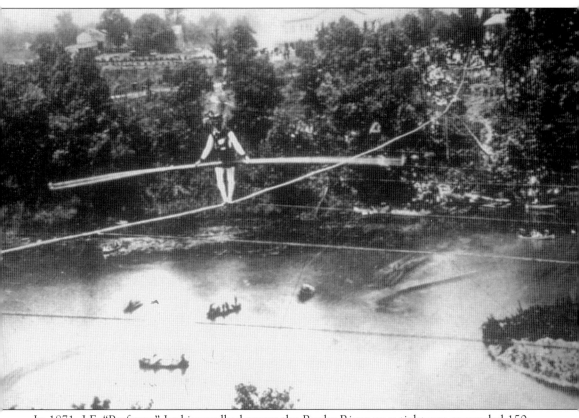

In 1871, J.F. "Professor" Jenkins walked across the Rocky River on a tightrope suspended 150 feet above the river. The length of the rope was 900 feet. This was probably a stunt to promote the Rocky River Dummy Railroad and the Cliff/Murch House. The Silverthorn Tavern can be seen in the background of the photograph above and to the left of Jenkins. Professor Jenkins had crossed the Niagara River Gorge two years earlier using a bicycle-like contraption on a tightrope. (Photograph Courtesy of Lakewood Historical Society.)

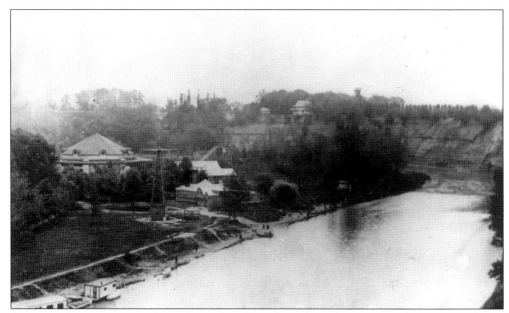

Scenic Park amusement park was located in the valley where the Metro Parks boat launch and park are today. The park had a car suspended on a cable that carried passengers across to a boathouse on the Rocky River side of the river. (Photograph Courtesy of Lakewood Historical Society.)

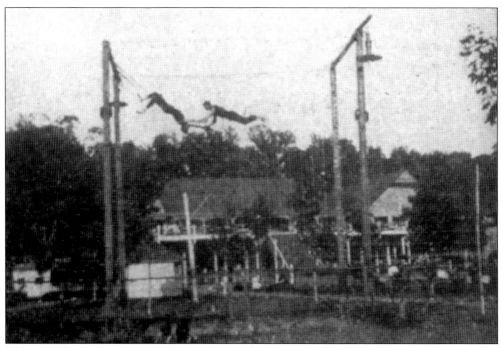

The park also had a 700-yard-long bicycle track, Ferris wheels, and performing trapeze artists. Liquor was sold in the park until 1905, when the sale of liquor in Lakewood was prohibited. In 1906 the park became Lincoln Park, and in 1917 it was sold to the city of Lakewood. (Photograph Courtesy of Lakewood Historical Society.)

Two

AROUND TOWN
IN THE OLD DAYS

Businesses in Rocky River grew up around the Silverthorn Tavern on Blount Street, as the east end of Lake Road was known for many years. This street, along with Old Detroit Road, which was known as North Ridge Road, was the heart of Rocky River. Some of the businesses such as the Silverthorn Tavern supported the tourist or resort trade. Grocery stores, lumberyards, hardware stores, feed stores, bakeries, and more supported the growing number of people who settled in the area permanently. While Lakewood was known for its orchards, Rocky River became known for its greenhouses and truck farms. These supplied vegetables to local grocers and to the markets in Cleveland.

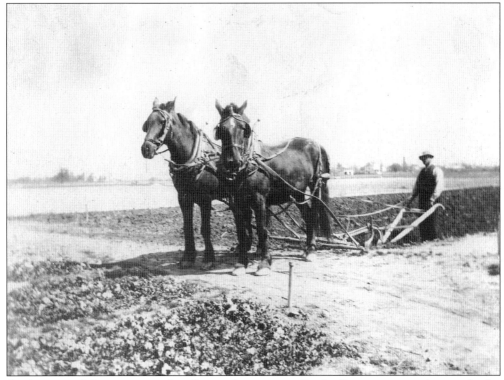

At the turn of the century and well into the twenties, Rocky River was a rural town. In the photograph above, Fred Schneider plows his fields located along Northview Avenue.

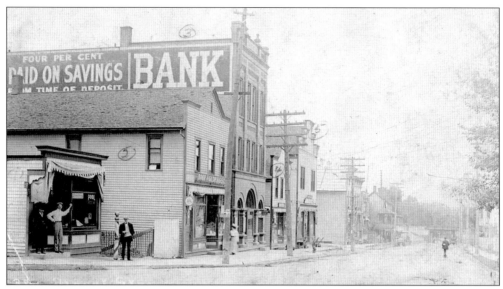

This photograph from the early 1900s shows businesses on the upper part of Blount Street, now Lake Road, looking north towards the railroad crossing. The Silverthorn Tavern was on the right, or east, side of the road. Businesses on the other side, from left to right are John Gall's Barbershop, Boore's (drugstore?), First National Bank of Rocky River, Schwartz's Bake Shop, and Ingersoll's Hardware on the corner of North Ridge, or Old Detroit Road.

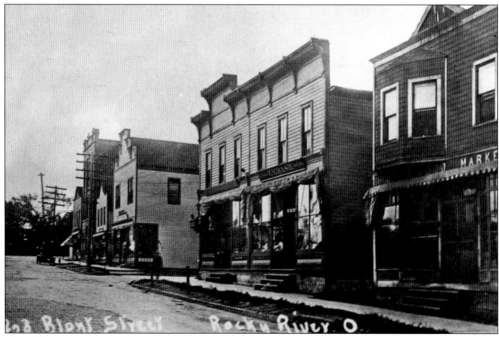

This photograph, taken at the same time as the previous one, shows Blount Street looking uphill, or south. Ingersoll's Hardware is the third building from the right, on the southwest corner of Detroit Road. The second building from the right is a grocery and dry goods store, which changed hands several times at the turn of the 19th century. (Photograph Courtesy of Rocky River Historical Society.)

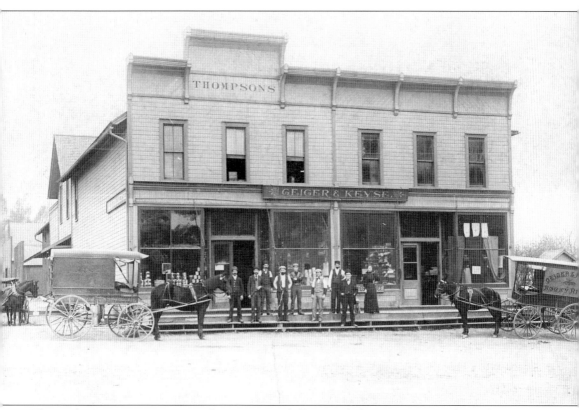

This is the grocery store seen in the previous uphill view of Blount Street. At the end of the 19th century, the store was run by the partnership of Geiger and Keyse. The post office was located for a time in one corner of this store. (Photograph Courtesy of Rocky River Historical Society.)

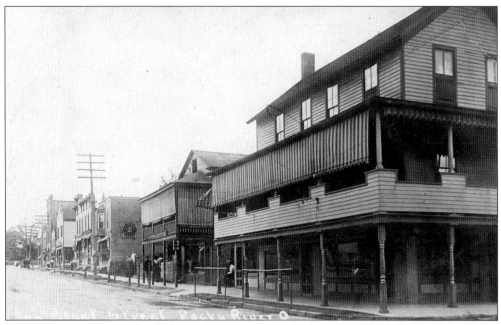

This is the entire west side of Blount Street, taken at the bottom of the hill. The Silverthorn Tavern, unseen, is on the east side of the street. The building on the corner is White's Saloon. The second building from right is Kennedy's Saloon.

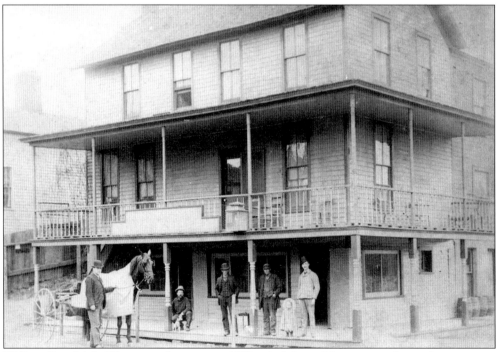

William Randolph White was the owner of White's Saloon. He is pictured at right wearing a light suit. An old-fashioned streetlight is hanging above his head. (Photograph Courtesy of Rocky River Historical Society.)

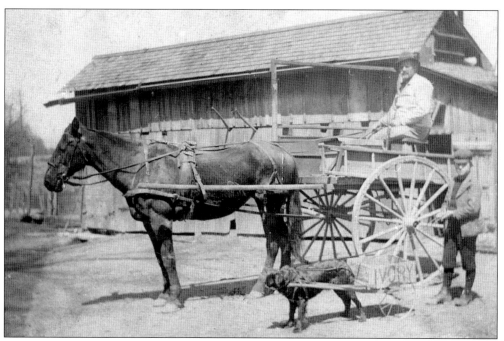

This is Jacob Berkemer, the lamplighter in Rocky River at the end of the 19th century. His son, Murray, is standing behind the small wagon harnessed to a dog. (Photograph Courtesy of Rocky River Historical Society.)

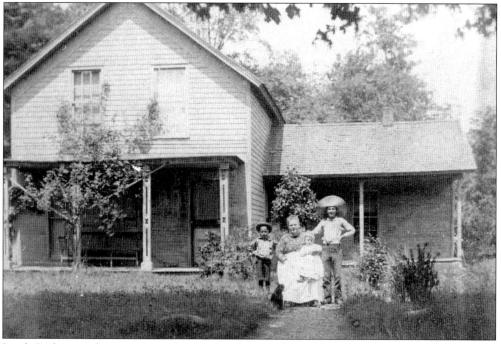

Jacob Berkemer's house was on Detroit Road, west of the downtown area. In this photo from the early 1890s, Mrs. Berkemer poses with son Murray in her lap and two neighbor boys. (Photograph Courtesy of Rocky River Historical Society.)

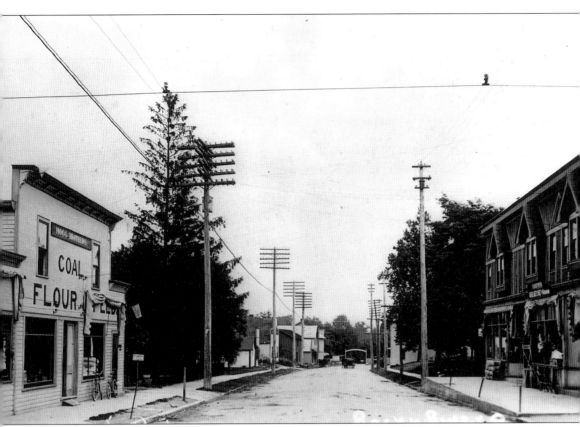

This photographic postcard shows North Ridge Road (Old Detroit) looking east towards the Silverthorn at the beginning of the 20th century. The gateway to the tavern shown in the next photo can be seen at the end of the road. On the left is the Hogg Brothers' Coal, Flour, and Feed store. With so many greenhouses in Rocky River, coal was big business. Greenhouses used coal to generate heat and to make steam to sterilize the soil.

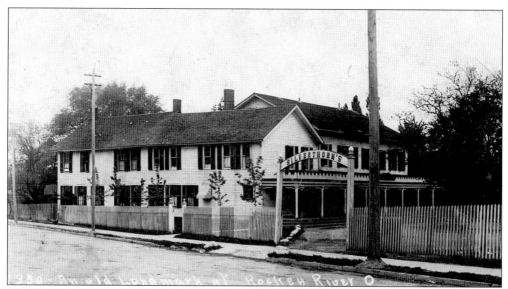

The Silverthorn was also known as an inn or hotel. A June 4, 1860 article in the *Plain Dealer* had this to say about the hospitality there: "Rocky River is a popular retreat with Clevelanders in summer time, Silverthorn's Hotel where a luxurious dinner can be prepared on fifteen minutes notice, being a bright and shining feature among the manifold attractions."

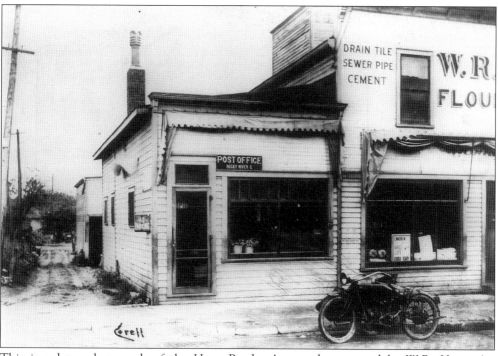

This is a later photograph of the Hogg Brothers' store, here owned by W.R. Hoag. An advertisement for the business in the 1925 Rocky River High School Yearbook, the *Riverlet*, simply states: "Coal, Concrete Block, Sand, Top Soil and Supplies." The post office was in this building from 1936 until it was torn down around 1940. (Photograph Courtesy of Cleveland State University Special Collections.)

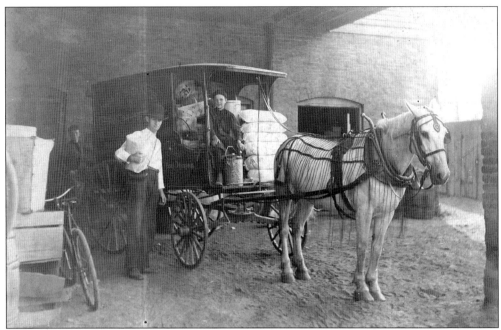

This is the delivery wagon of Jim Wilson's grocery, which was located on Old Detroit Road. Jim is standing by the wagon, Otto Wilson is behind the wagon, and Willis Rumbaugh is sitting in the wagon. (Photograph Courtesy of Rocky River Historical Society.)

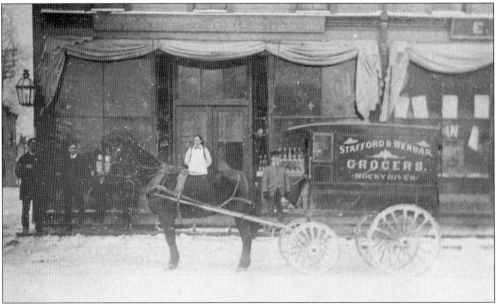

The delivery wagon of Stafford and Wenban Grocers stands in front of its store on the north corner of Detroit and Blount. Earl Stafford and Sion Wenban bought the business in the late 1890s from Geiger and Keyse, whose store is pictured earlier in this chapter. Sion Wenban was the second mayor of Rocky River, serving from 1913 to 1917. He was also head of the Rocky River Basket Company on Lake Road, which supplied baskets to all the greenhouses and truck farms. (Photograph Courtesy of Rocky River Historical Society.)

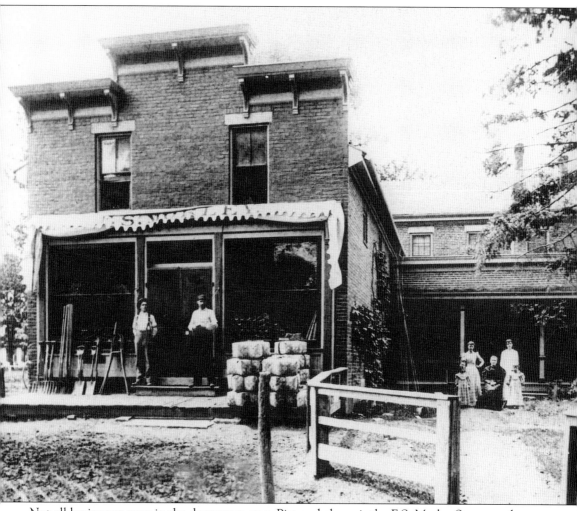

Not all businesses were in the downtown area. Pictured above is the F.S. Morley Store, on the northwest corner of Center Ridge and Wooster roads. This store was originally known as Phinney's Corners. Benjamin Phinney was the first owner and was an early postmaster of the western part of Rockport around the time of the Civil War. The store under both Phinney and Morley sold groceries, notions, farm supplies and tools, all of which could be delivered by horse and wagon. (Photograph Courtesy of Rocky River Historical Society.)

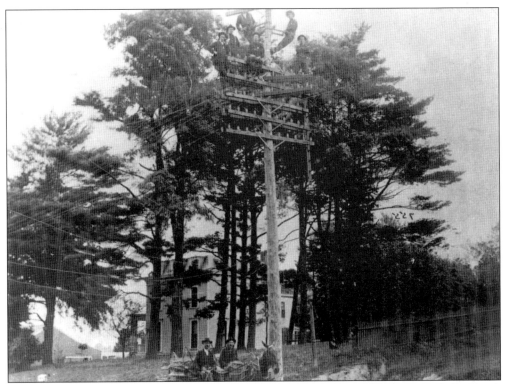

This house was located on the east side of Wooster Road, to the north of Center Ridge Road. The original house on this property had been a stop for a stagecoach route that ran along Wooster. Thomas and Emily Macbeth, whose names are associated with the founding of the Rocky River Public Library, bought the property in 1903. This photograph was taken some time after 1900, the year when the town gave permission to the Cuyahoga Telephone Company to erect poles and wires. (Photograph Courtesy of Rocky River Public Library.)

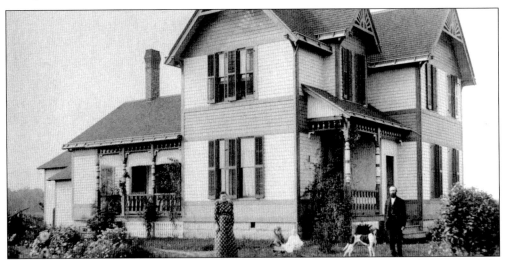

The Salomon Pease House stood on the south side of Center Ridge, across from where River Oaks is today, in the vicinity of Pease Drive. This photograph, circa 1893, shows Salomon Pease II with wife, daughter, and dog. (Photograph Courtesy of Rocky River Historical Society.)

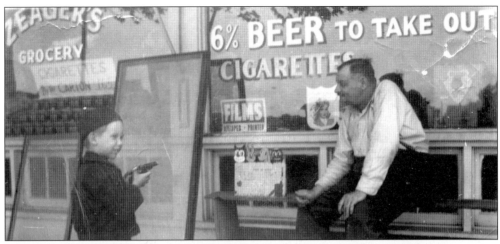

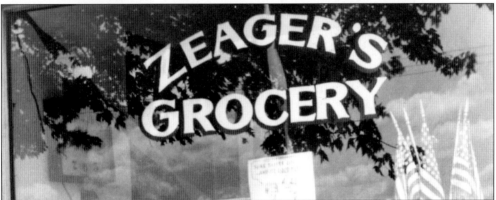

The Zeager Grocery was located on the northwest corner of Center Ridge and Northview on the Zeager farm. Besides selling groceries, this store sold fireworks until a law was passed in Rocky River forbidding the sale of such in city limits. The managers of the store were able to meet the fireworks needs of the town's residents by placing a small stand a short distance west of the store, near where Dale Avenue is located today. The area west of the store was in Goldwood Township, which had no laws against the sale of fireworks. The Goldwood area detached itself from Rocky River in 1910 and was its own township until 1926, when part of it was annexed back into Rocky River.

This was the Zeager Farm, at 20630 Center Ridge, west of the store. The land was sold to the town in 1926 to allow a new school to be built on the property. Instead of building a school here, the town built Goldwood School farther west along Center Ridge Road in 1927. Rocky River built the school there as a condition for the annexation of Goldwood Township.

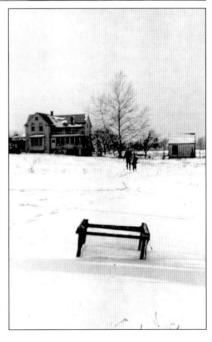

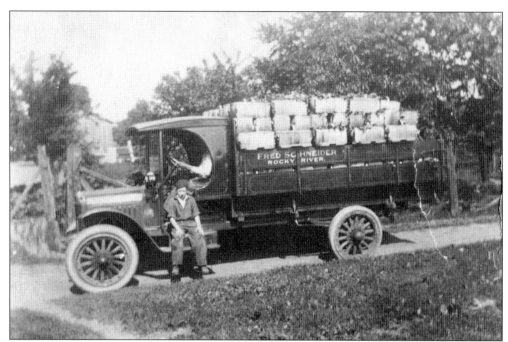

Farmers in Rocky River sold their produce to area stores. They also traveled to the West Side Market to sell their goods. For this reason the farms were called truck farms, since they trucked their vegetables and flowers themselves. Fred Schneider farmed much of the land that now comprises the athletic fields of Rocky River High School.

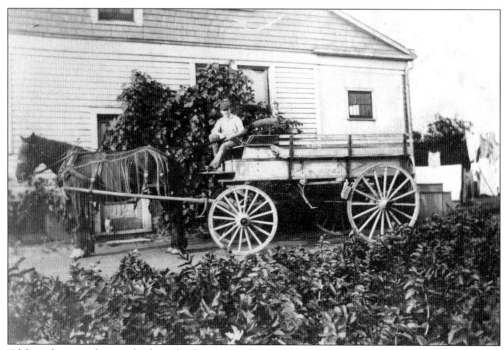

Although many farmers had trucks, horses, and carts, they still did a lot of the work. Here, Bill Schneider and Dolly are ready to go to work.

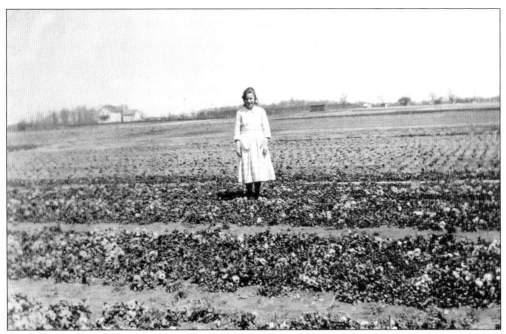

Elsie Schneider poses in her father's fields in this photograph. As the eldest, Elsie left school in order to help work on the farm and care for younger siblings. Her father bought her a camera and she used it to take pictures of the family farm, family members, and friends.

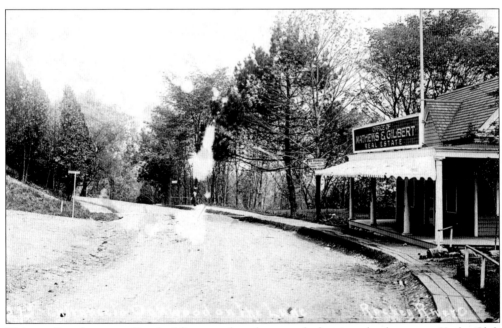

This small real estate office building stood at the top of what is today known as Yacht Club Drive. Mathews and Gilbert sold realty in the area known as Oakwood-on-the-Lake. This was the name of the property that belonged to Daniel P. Eells, owner of the point at the mouth of the Rocky River (formerly Tisdale Point) plus 150 adjoining acres. Mathews & Gilbert purchased the property after Eells' death in 1903.

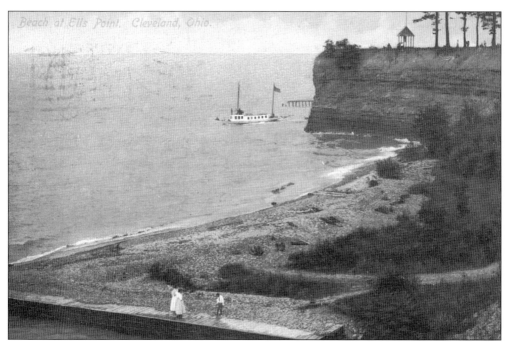

This postcard shows the point at the mouth of the Rocky River, here called Eells Point, in the Oakwood-on-the-Lake property. In 1893, the Eells home that stood on the point burned down. There was no organized fire department in Rocky River at the time.

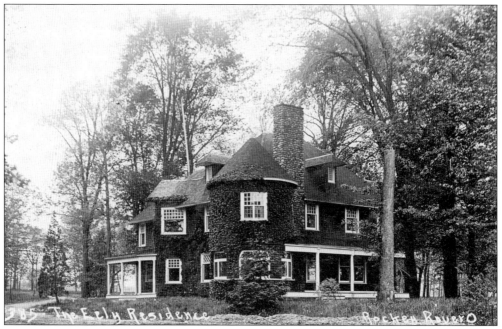

Eells built a second house on his property after his first one burned down. This house still stands today on Frazier Drive. The post card above mistakenly identifies the house as the "Eely" residence. Mathews and Gilbert later used this postcard as an advertisement for the sale of the house.

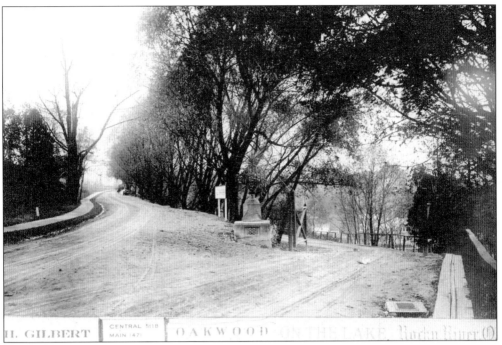

This is a promotional post card for H. Gilbert, of Mathews and Gilbert Real Estate. The view shows Yacht Club Drive on the right and Frazier Drive going off to the left. In 1908, four streets in the Oakwood allotment—Frazier, Kensington Oval, Argyle Oval, and Buckingham Road— were approved by the city for sewer and water service.

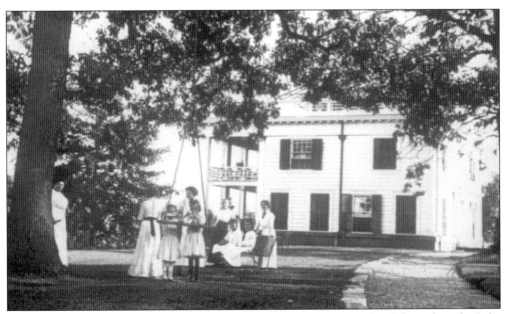

This is the Van Dorn home, circa 1910, built at 19420 Frazier Drive in the Oakwood-on-the-Lake area. The Van Dorn Iron Works Company was at one time the largest producer of jail cells in the United States. The company started working with steel in time to profit from the automobile boom in the early 20th century. (Photograph Courtesy of Lakewood Historical Society.)

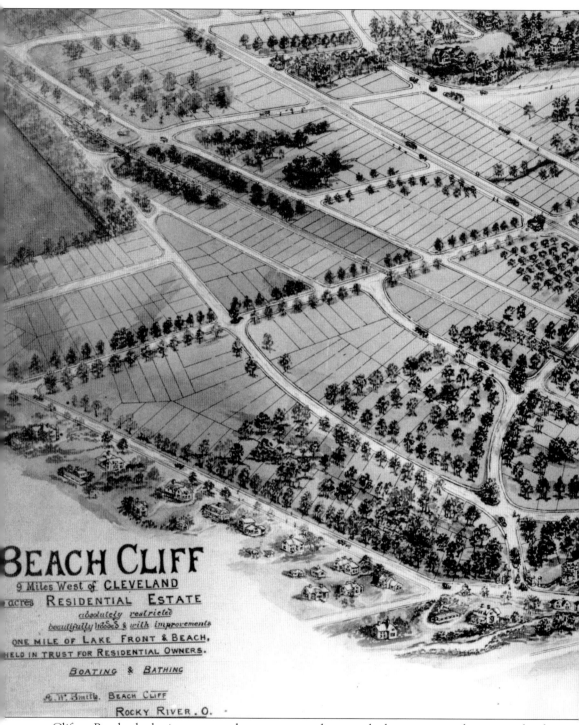

BEACH CLIFF
9 Miles West of CLEVELAND
acres RESIDENTIAL ESTATE
absolutely restricted
beautifully wooded & with improvements
ONE MILE OF LAKE FRONT & BEACH,
HELD IN TRUST FOR RESIDENTIAL OWNERS.

BOATING & BATHING

A. W. Smith. BEACH CLIFF
ROCKY RIVER. O.

Clifton Beach, the businessman and congressman who owned a large estate with over a mile of lakefront property, died in 1902. The real estate company that developed his land called the development Beach Cliff. Above is a promotional map of the area showing the proposed layout of the development. The road running along the bottom of the map is Detroit Road. The Rocky

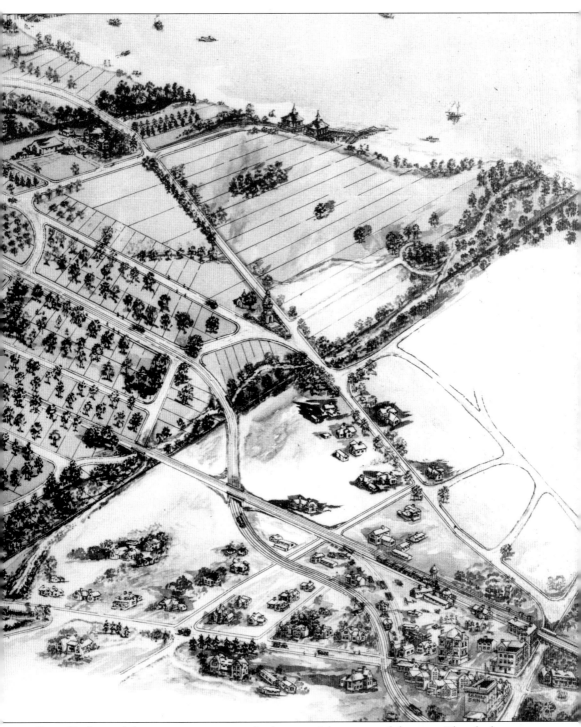

River Bridge and downtown area are on the bottom right corner of the map. The clock tower at Lake and Avalon can be seen above, approximately in the middle of the right side of this page. It was built by the developer to serve as an entrance marker to the Beach Cliff Estates.

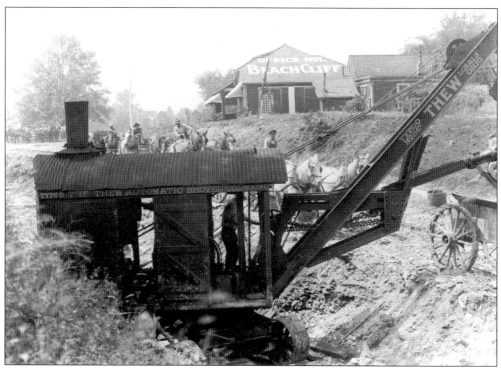

An early phase of the construction in Beach Cliff Estates is seen above in this circa 1910 photograph. The location is unknown.

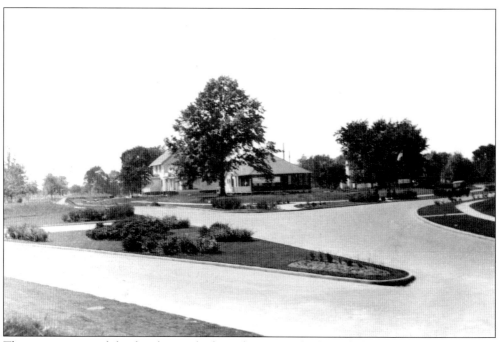

These were some of the first houses built at the east end of Beachcliff Boulevard and Frazier Drive. Batterson Boulevard is the road on the left.

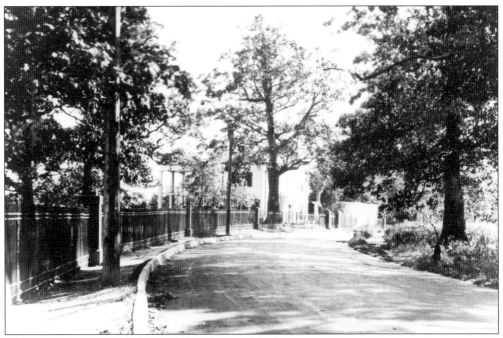

This is another view of the Van Dorn home. The house standing on Frazier today is not the same house. The original house burned down in 1991. The new house was built to resemble the 1906 original.

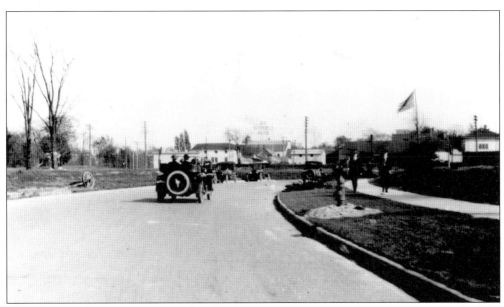

This photograph captures a time when Rocky River was a new and growing town. World War I and the Great Depression were more than a decade away. The sign on the Guardian Bank on Blount Street can be discerned in the background, offering 4% on savings. The Guardian Bank can be seen in the various photographs of Blount Street in this chapter. The car above is probably driving along Beachcliff Boulevard.

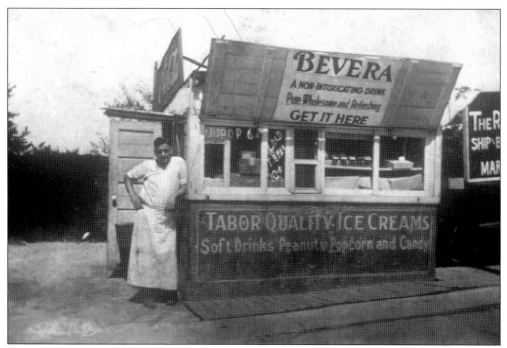

As Rocky River was growing, changes were occurring in the downtown area. Peter and Steve Sougianis ran this refreshment stand on the northwest corner end of the Detroit Road Bridge. This photo, circa 1918, shows Steve Sougianis manning the stand. The Sougianis brothers came over to the US from Greece. (Photograph Courtesy of Lakewood Historical Society.)

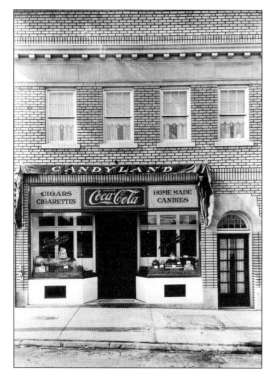

In 1926, the Sougianis brothers opened Candyland in the building across from their stand, where the restaurant Salmon Dave's is today, across from the Westlake Hotel. The store was the site of the first mechanical soda fountain in Cuyahoga County. The Sougianis brothers made syrups for sodas and chocolates from Greek recipes. An ad in the 1925 Riverlet boasts: "Candyland. The Home of Sweets. Where Quality and Sanitation Reign Supreme." (Photograph Courtesy of Rocky River Historical Society.)

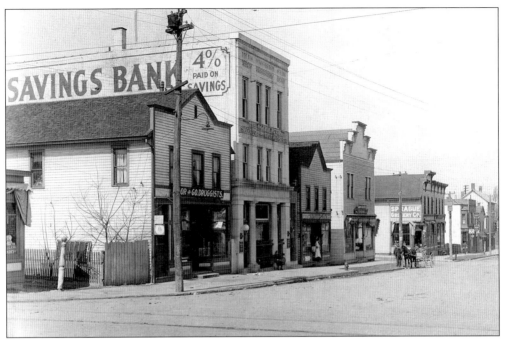

This circa 1920 photograph of Blount Street is taken from a similar point as that of the turn-of-the-century view that opened this chapter. Some changes have been made to the bank (the tall building) and the street has been improved. The grocery on the corner of Blount and Detroit, formerly Geiger & Keyse, and then Stafford & Wenban, was under the ownership of Mr. Sprague at the time of this photograph. (Photograph Courtesy of Rocky River Historical Society.)

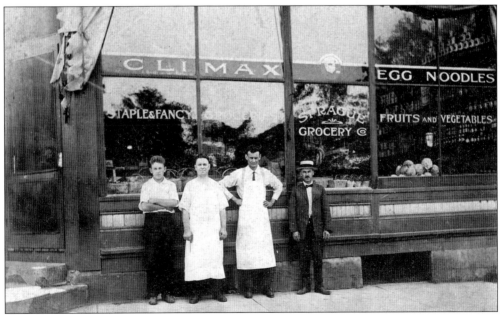

The Sprague Grocery stood on the north corner of Detroit Road and Lake. This was at least the third grocery to occupy this building. (Photograph Courtesy of Rocky River Historical Society.)

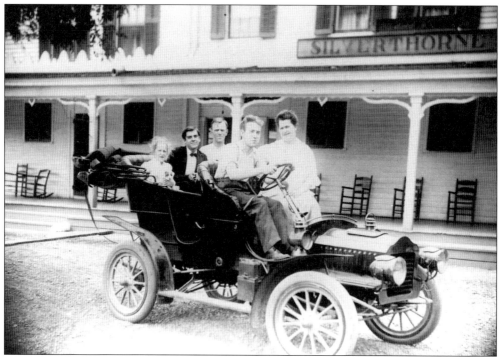

This photograph was taken in 1905 in front of the Silverthorn Tavern. Alfred Morton is at the wheel of the car. Mrs. R.S. Morton is at his side and the other people are unidentified. The chairs on the porch of the Silverthorn (spelled Silverthorne on the sign) bear mute testimony to the important role the tavern played in the social life of the town.

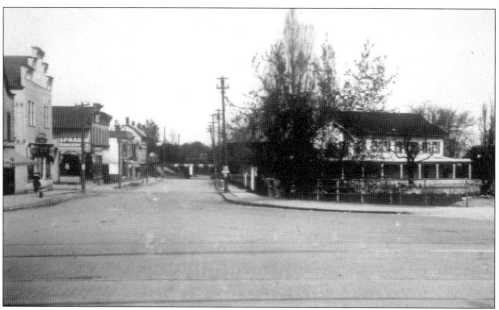

This is probably one of the last photos taken of Blount Street and the Silverthorn. The tavern was torn down around 1920 in order to make way for the Westlake Hotel. (Photograph Courtesy of Lakewood Historical Society.)

Three
WRITING, READING, AND RELIGION

It is hard to say exactly where and how many schools existed in Rocky River before 1880. By some accounts, the first school was located on Detroit Road, about a mile west from the river. A second school, located near the corner of Detroit and Wagar Roads, was known as the Dean school, as it sat on Dean family property. An early school stood near the corner of Wooster and Detroit. Yet another school stood near the northeast corner of Center Ridge and Northview Avenue. This last school is the only one indicated on the Rockport map from the Titus, Simmons, & Titus Atlas of Cuyahoga County, 1874. (See page 6.)

Elementary school education was somewhat well established in Rocky River by 1880, when a one-story structure was built on Wooster Road near Center Ridge Road. It housed students from 1880 until 1902. In 1892 a high school was organized in this building, with the first class of five students graduating in 1897. Rocky River continued to offer high school classes until 1909, using either Wooster School or Beach School for classes.

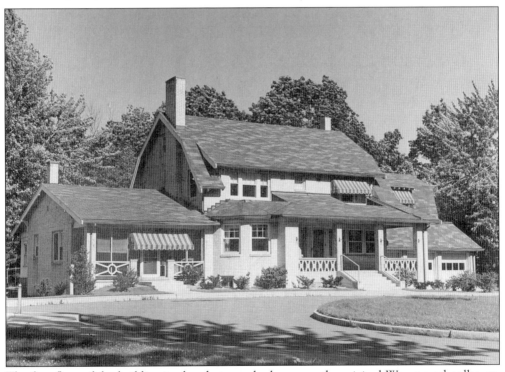

The first floor of the building in the photograph above was the original Wooster schoolhouse. It eventually was turned into a home and was known as the Baker House. Later, the house was used by the Rocky River Board of Education for offices. (Photograph Courtesy of Rocky River Board of Education.)

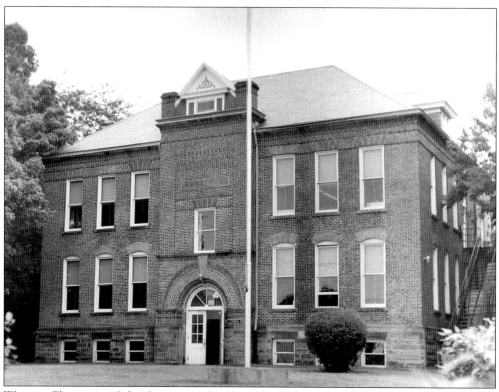

Wooster Elementary School was completed in 1902. The original building was a four-room, one-story structure. It was expanded in 1922 and 1945 and consisted of six rooms and an auditorium. After the present-day Wooster School was built in 1955, the old Wooster School became known as the Wooster Annex and housed the Board of Education offices. The building was destroyed in 1990–1991. Today a commemorative sign stands on the location of the old Wooster School. (Photograph Courtesy of Rocky River Board of Education.)

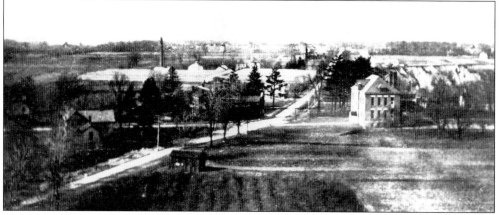

This is an aerial view looking south down Wooster Road in the early 20th century. Wooster School can be seen at right. Across from the school, on the corner of Center Ridge and Wooster, and behind some trees, is Morley's Store, as described on page 31. On the west side of Wooster, south of the store, are the Gasser family greenhouses. (Photograph Courtesy of Rocky River Public Library.)

This is of one of the first classes to attend the 1902 Wooster School. The photograph at right was taken circa 1904. (Photograph Courtesy of Rocky River Historical Society.)

The photograph below of the younger classes at Beach School was taken circa 1901. At that time there was no kindergarten in Rocky River. Students started school at the age of six years, when they entered the first grade. (Photograph Courtesy of Rocky River Historical Society.)

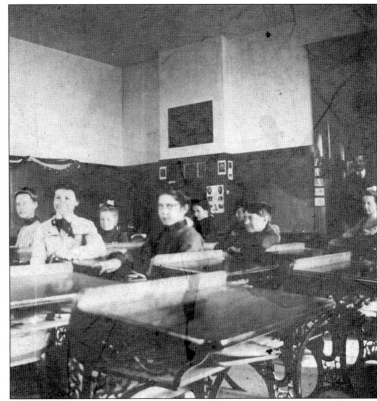

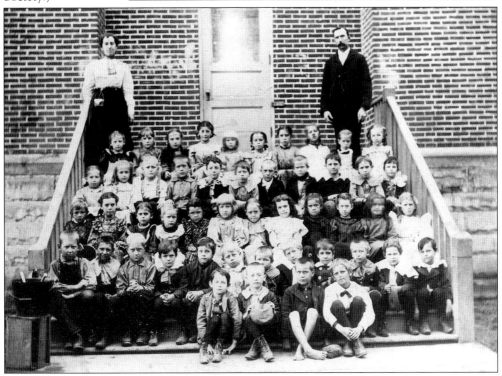

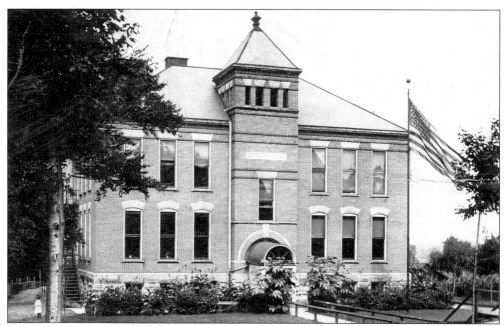

Beach Elementary School was built in 1897 on the corner of Detroit Road and Morewood Parkway. The school was named in honor of Clifford Beach, who donated 3 acres for the building and school grounds. Morewood was not developed at that time, and the school was surrounded by woods on the west and north sides. It was the first large, two-story brick school built in Rocky River.

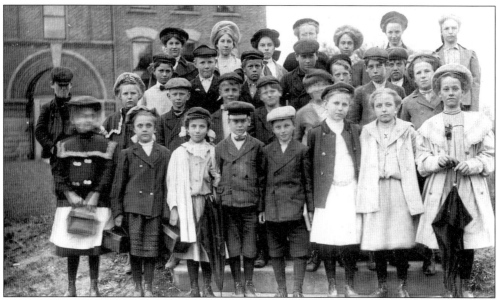

These Beach School students appear to be in about the fifth or sixth grade. Their classroom would have been on the second floor, as the younger grades were on the first floor. The lunchroom was in the basement of the school. Most students brought their lunches to school and ate them there. In the winter, mothers would come in and make hot soup for student lunches. (Photograph Courtesy of Rocky River Public Library.)

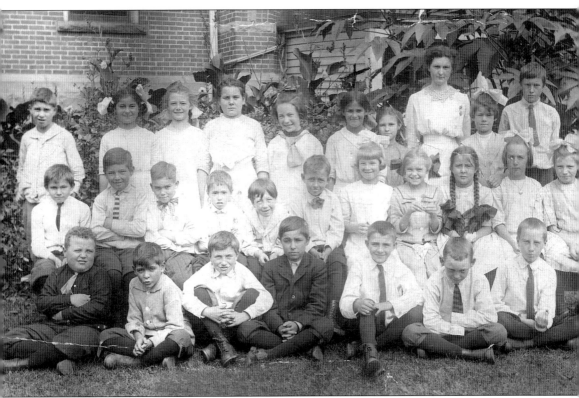

This is a photograph of Mary E. Case's class at Beach School, taken circa 1912. The students are probably in the fourth grade. The classmates, as identified by Frieda Schneid Pitts, from left to right, are as follows: (front row) Louis Wearsh, unidentified, Albert Shearer, unidentified, Louis Kozenik, George Hoy, and Hans Dixon.; (middle row) Howard Gerbrand, unidentified, Norman Reed, Francis Stevens, unidentified, Reginald Clevett, Robert Stofer, Cristina Miller, Norma Arff, Lucille Price, Helen Codding, and Agnes Hansen; (back row) Adelbert Petersen, unidentified, Florence Butts, unidentified, Marie Gravatt, Frieda Pitts, Pearl Decks, Mary Case (teacher), Helen Ingersoll, and Harvey Stepler.

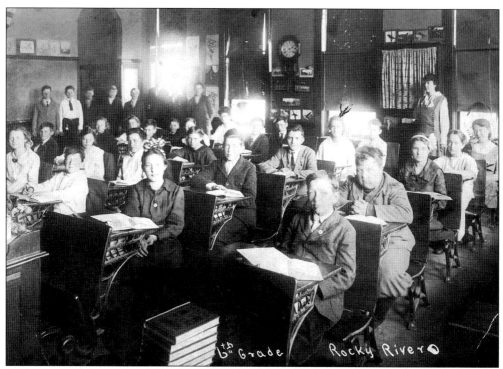

This is a photograph of the same class in the sixth grade at Beach School, circa 1914. The girl in the fourth seat back in the second row is Frieda Schneider.

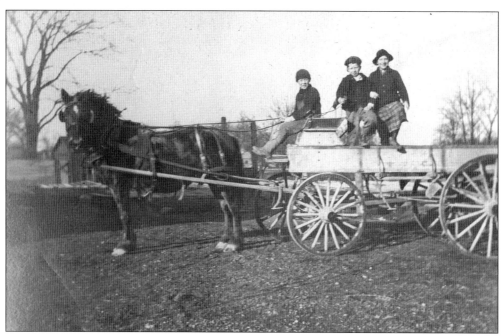

The Schneider children lived on Northview Avenue and attended Beach School. In this photograph from the early 1920s William, Frederick, and Gertrude Schneider appear to be happy not to be in school.

50

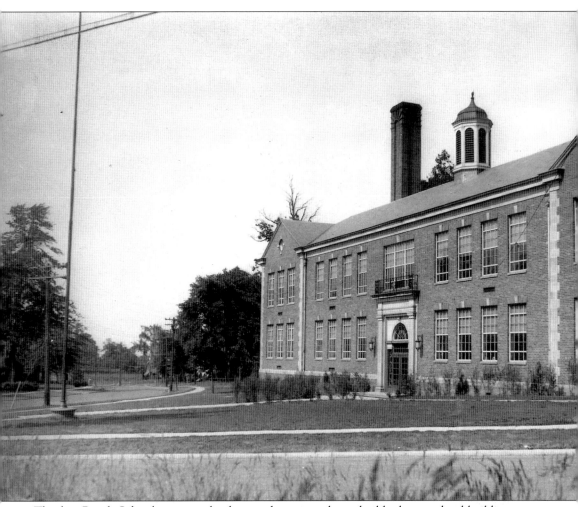

The first Beach School was completely torn down in order to build a larger school building on the same property. The building shown above was completed in 1931. In 1963, a large addition was built on to the east side of the building. (Photograph Courtesy of the Cleveland Press Archives at Cleveland State University.)

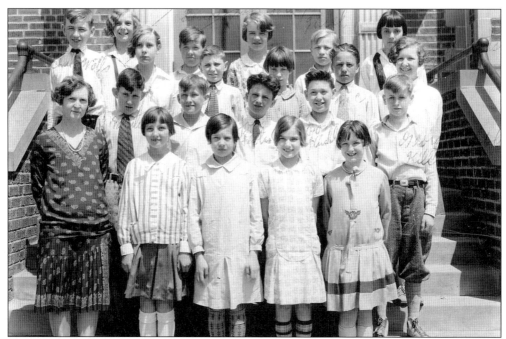

Kensington School opened for its first school year in 1927–1928. The school was needed to meet the growing population of the Beach Cliff area, north of the railroad tracks. The first sixth grade class to attend the school is pictured above, from left to right, as follows: (first row) Miss Maizie Case (teacher), Jean Yost, Helen Simoncic, unidentified, and Nancy Eady; (second row) John Weitz, unidentified, unidentified, Don Hinckley, and George Keppler; (third row) Charles Watts, Ruth Winsper, unidentified, unidentified, Robert Bowles, and Dorothy Mitzel; (fourth row) Louise Snelling, William Ritchie, Dorothy Gundersen, John Heil, and Betty Deemer. A note on this old photograph says that George Keppler died in World War II.

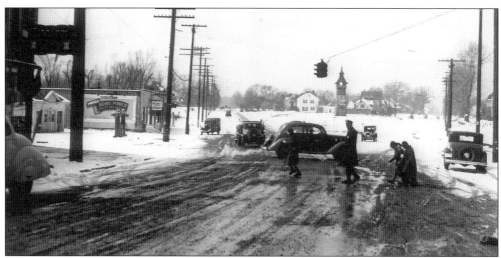

Lake Road in front of Kensington School looked like this in the 1930s. These students are probably crossing over to the Newell family's deli for a snack. The clock tower in the background was built by the developer of the Beach Cliff Estates around 1912. (Photograph Courtesy of the Cleveland Press Archives at Cleveland State University.)

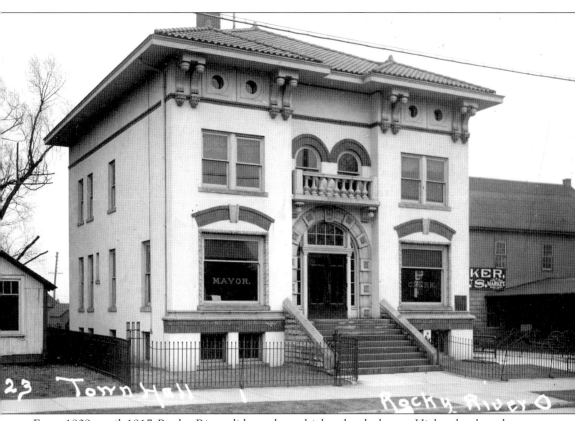

From 1909 until 1917 Rocky River did not have high school classes. High school students attended schools in either Lakewood or Cleveland. In 1917, Cleveland and Lakewood stopped accepting students from Rocky River into their high schools due to overcrowding. In that same year, 44 River students started attending high school in the former city hall on Old Detroit Avenue. The following is an excerpt from the tongue-in-cheek Class History of 1921 written by class member Wynne Hastings, who started high school in the city hall:

> For our debut into high school the town hall made a very quiet, peaceful place at least. Aside from a blacksmith shop next door, a busy street in front, a railroad yard in the rear, two crossings for the interurban to toot at reasonably close and an occasional hilarious jailbird just below us, there wasn't a thing in the world to distract us from our studies. We soon got so interested in our work, however, that this didn't bother us at all.

(Photograph Courtesy of Dugan's Barbershop.)

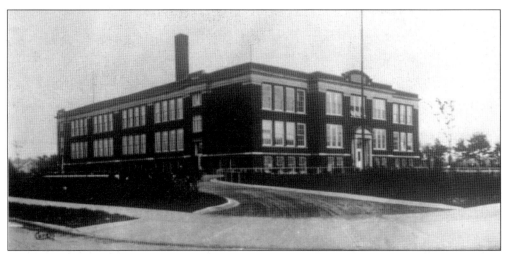

In 1919, Rocky River high school students moved into their own new school building. Originally the Rocky River High School, this building stood until very recently on the northwest corner of Lakeview and Riverview Avenues. Construction on the school started in 1917 and the building welcomed its first students, grades 7–12, in 1919. In 1950, the building became the Junior High School for grades 7–8, as the upper grades attended a new high school, still used today, on the corner of Detroit and Wagar Roads. Over the years, a variety of additions were made to the original high school, including a 1976 addition that ruined the distinguished façade on Lakeview Avenue. The entire building was demolished in 2000 to make way for the new Rocky River Middle School. (Photograph Courtesy of Lakewood Historical Society.)

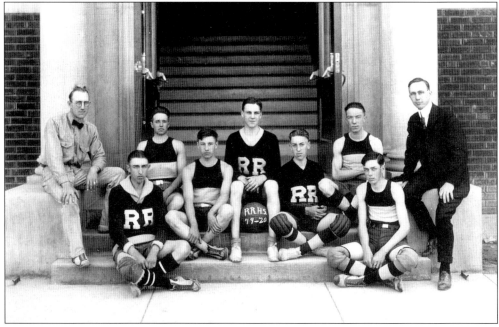

Rocky River High School had about 150 students and 12 teachers in its first complete school year in the new school building, when this team photo was taken. By 1927–1928, there were over 400 students enrolled in the school, allowing for first string and second string basketball teams. (Photograph Courtesy of Rocky River Public Library.)

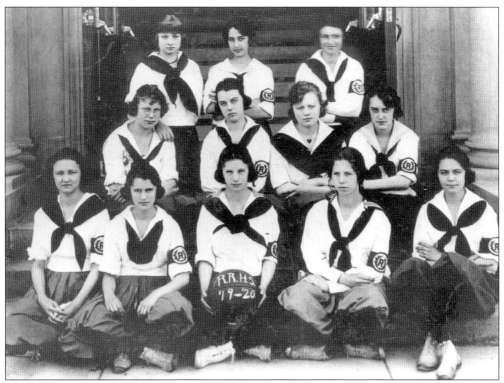

After 1928, high school girls were not permitted to participate in athletic events with other schools. This was a common restriction among most Cleveland-area high schools. Until that time the Rocky River girls did well in inter-school competitions. (Photograph Courtesy of Rocky River Public Library.)

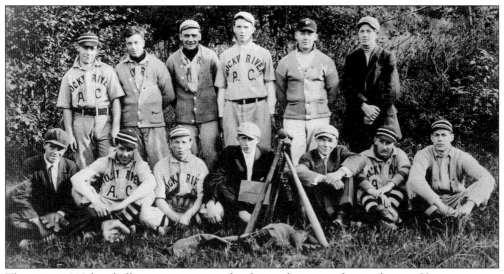

This circa 1912 baseball team was not a school team but part of a city league. However, some of the players appear school-aged. Unfortunately, the players are unidentified except for three in the first row: second from left is Ed Walchli, third from left is James "Bud" Bowles, and first from right is Frank Walchli.

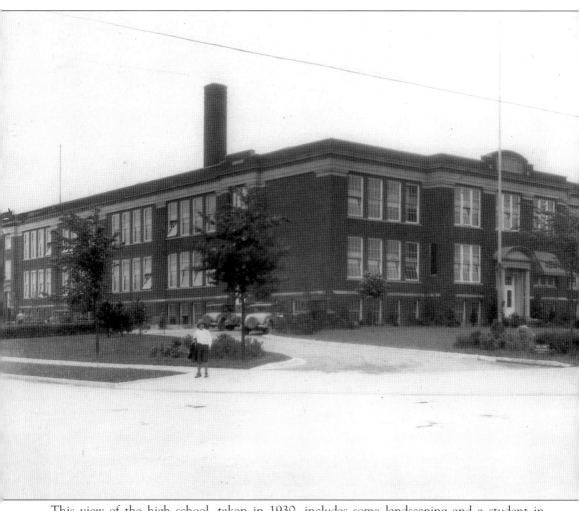

This view of the high school, taken in 1930, includes some landscaping and a student in knickers, probably from the younger classes. Faculty roadsters can be seen behind the student in the parking area. (Photograph Courtesy of Cleveland Press Archives at Cleveland State University.)

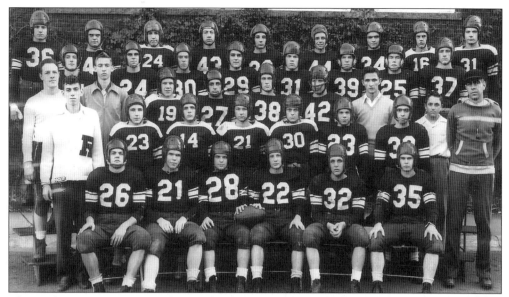

The Rocky River Pirates were the Southwestern Conference Football Champions of 1948. They are, from left to right, pictured as follows: (front row) Dave McCollam, John Saunders, Dick Killius, Bill Henning, Dick Baller, and Tom Hardesty; (second row) Manager Roger Herrett, Andy Cheek, Tom Black, Ken Yablinski, Dick Rothrock, John Schurman, and Coach Randall Motts; (third row) Assistant Coach Vince Gandolfi, Assistant Manager Bob Pienkowski, Don Kmetz, Lou Tasse, Ned Beach, Dick Viers, Assistant Manager Blair Algie, and Assistant Manager Don Tasse; (fourth row) Scott Minner, Kirk Free, Bob Bowers, Bud Kinsley, Ralph Zowad, Tom Hague, Bruce Lydrickson, and Jim Horton; (fifth row) Dick Broerman, Bob Eckhardt, Tom Gross, Ralph Greenman, Fred Lamb, Dick Rouce, Dick Berneike, Don Welshans, and Jim Chandler. (Photograph Courtesy of Cleveland Press Archives at Cleveland State University.)

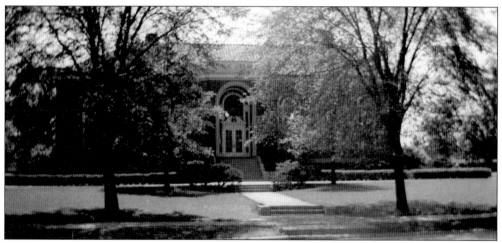

In 1924, the Cuyahoga County Library started a free library in the high school building on Lakeview Avenue. This library was open to the public as well as students. In the same year, a group of citizens interested in having a public library in Rocky River organized a Rocky River Library Association. In 1926, a board of trustees was elected to oversee the formation of a public library. The original entrance of the Rocky River Public Library was a grand one off of Riverview Avenue. (Photograph Courtesy of Rocky River Public Library.)

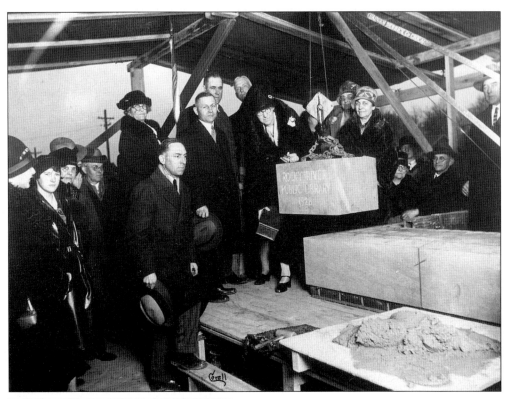

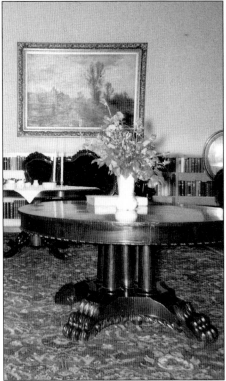

The cornerstone for the new Rocky River Public Library was laid on February 4, 1928. Inside it were copies of Cleveland newspapers for February 3, 1928, pictures of Rocky River, and a history of the library movement in Rocky River. In the photograph above, from left to right, are the following: (up front) Ida Belle Jacobs, Margaret Pierce, Margaret Relph, and Bertram Relph; (on the steps) May Dean (Trustee), and Ralph Richards (Trustee); (on the platform) H.M. Jacobs (Trustee), W.R. Hoag (Trustee), Rev. Burr (Rockport), Emily Macbeth (Trustee filling cornerstone), Lilan Hastings, Miss Roena Ingham (Lakewood Librarian), Miss Linda Eastman (Cleveland Public Librarian), Elsie Cleverdon (Trustee), and D.C. Reed. (Photograph Courtesy of Rocky River Public Library.)

Sophia Schlather, wife of successful businessman and philanthropist Leonard Schlather, donated $100,000 to the Rocky River Public Library upon her death in 1956. This allowed the library to double its size. The Schlather Room in the library contained many gifts from the Schlathers, who were world travelers. (Photograph Courtesy of Rocky River Public Library.)

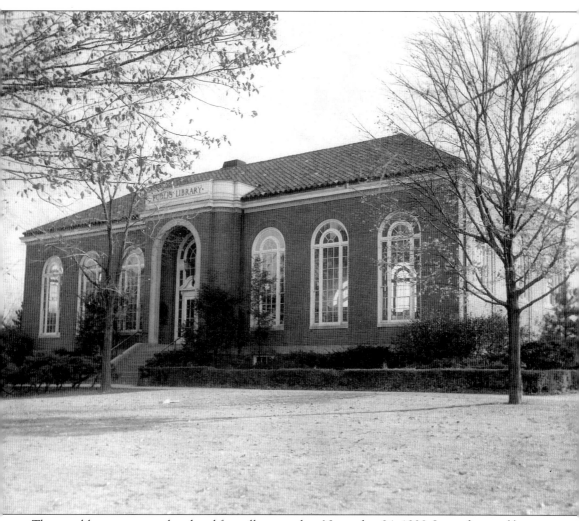

The new library was completed and formally opened on November 24, 1928. It was financed by a $60,000 bond issue and a $25,000 donation from Thomas and Emily Macbeth. (Photograph Courtesy of Cleveland Press Archives at Cleveland State University.)

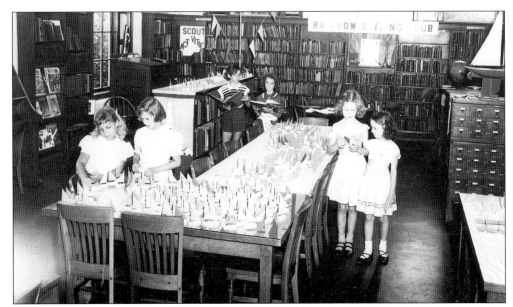

The children's room in the old library was in the northwest corner of the building, just to the left of the front door. This photo was taken in the 1950s. The windows and doors were opened on warm summer days, which was pleasant for the patrons but, perhaps, not good for the books. (Photograph Courtesy of Rocky River Public Library.)

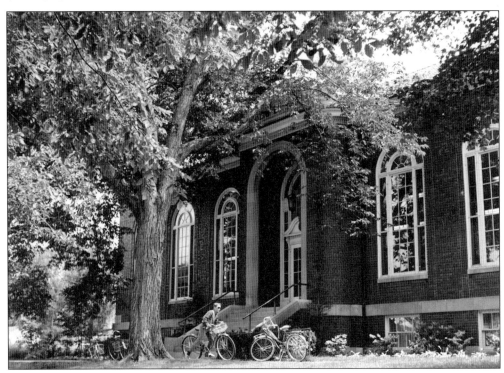

The library was centrally located. Many children could ride their bikes to it in the summertime. These bikes are parked by the front door on Riverview Avenue. (Photograph Courtesy of Rocky River Board of Education.)

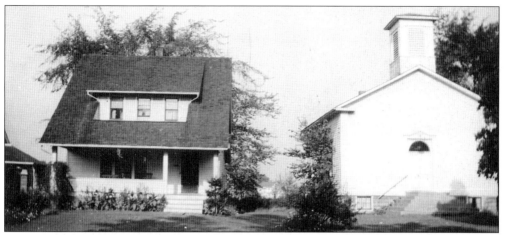

The Rockport Methodist Episcopal Church building shown above was built in 1847. Before the building was constructed, church services were held in the homes or barns of the members. Services were led by circuit riders, men who traveled from church to church for this purpose. The old church was located at 3300 Wooster Road. A newer brick church was built next to the old church in 1947. A 1940 *Cleveland Press* cartoon states that the Rockport Methodist Church is the oldest church west of the Cuyahoga River. The original church building is still standing and is the oldest building in Rocky River. (Photograph Courtesy of Rocky River Historical Society.)

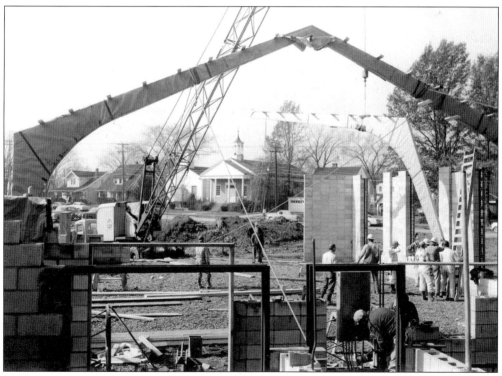

This photograph shows the original wooden church and the newer brick church during the construction of the present-day Rockport Methodist church building, which opened in 1963. The former church buildings are now occupied by the Buna Vestire Romanian Orthodox Church. (Photograph Courtesy of Rockport Methodist Church.)

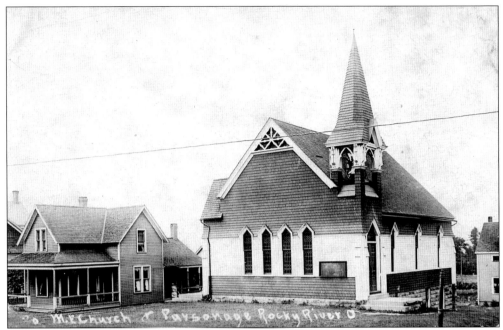

The Rocky River Methodist Episcopal Church was formed in 1885 by a group of women who called themselves the Willing Workers. They met in a small building on Eastlook Road. The building shown above was built on the corner of Detroit Road and Parsons Court in 1893. At that time there were 30 members in the church.

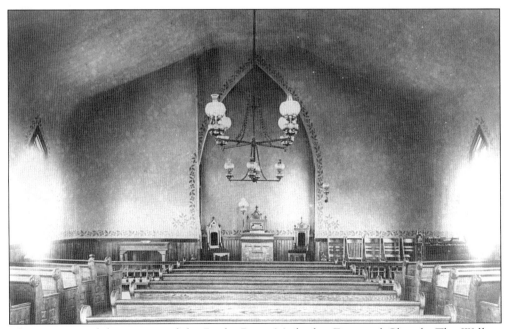

This is a view of the interior of the Rocky River Methodist Episcopal Church. The Willing Workers held fund-raising activities to build the new church. Generous donations from some prominent members of the community helped to make the church possible. (Photograph Courtesy of Rocky River Historical Society.)

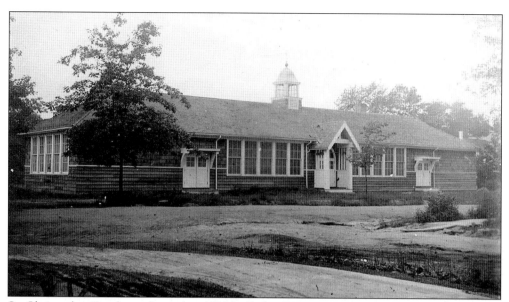

St. Christopher Parish was formed in 1922 by Father R. J. Patterson. The parish consisted of 35 families from the area of Rocky River, Bay Village, and Westlake. Services were first held in the old City Hall building on Detroit Road until a church could be built on property located at the southwest corner of Detroit and Lakeview Avenue. The building in the photograph above was completed in 1923. The first services were held in the new church on Palm Sunday, 1923. (Photograph Courtesy of St. Christopher Catholic Church.)

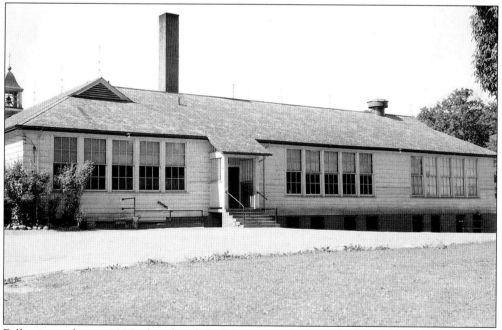

Following a fire in 1925, the church building was rebuilt, with the addition of four school classrooms. Seventeen children graduated from the first eighth grade class in 1934, taught by nuns from St. James Convent in Lakewood. (Photograph Courtesy of St. Christopher Catholic Church.)

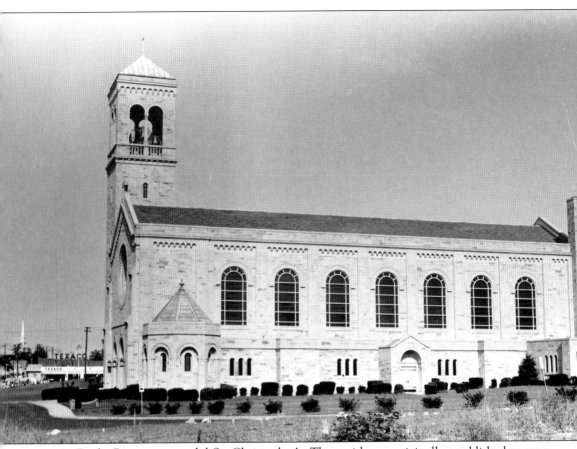

As Rocky River grew, so did St. Christopher's. The parish was originally established to serve the western section of Greater Cleveland, which included Bay Village and Westlake. By the 1940s, Bay had its own parish, and St. Christopher's was still growing. The new church building that still stands today was dedicated in 1953. (Photograph Courtesy of St. Christopher Catholic Church.)

Four
COWAN POTTERY

Rocky River was the home of Cowan Pottery from 1921 until 1931. The pottery produced at Cowan was called "artware"—objects of art that were practical. Cowan Pottery was and still is famous for its simple yet beautiful designs and unique glazes.

R. Guy Cowan was a ceramic artist whose work came to the attention of the Cleveland Chamber of Commerce in 1912. The Chamber recognized Cowan's artistic ability and thought it could bring Cleveland some welcome attention and prestige. With the help of the Chamber and art patrons, Cowan opened his first ceramic studio in 1912, on Nicholson Avenue in Lakewood. He stayed there until 1921, when the gas well that fired his kilns was depleted. He then moved his business to 19633 Lake Road, Rocky River.

In the years before the depression Cowan Pottery was turning out over 175,000 items a year. Artists designing for Cowan won awards at juried shows and exhibitions. However, the studio was not able to survive the Great Depression and closed in 1932 after selling off its inventory. R. Guy Cowan moved to New York and continued working as a ceramicist, but he never opened another studio. The work of the Cowan Pottery Studio can be seen today at the Cowan Pottery Museum in the Rocky River Public Library.

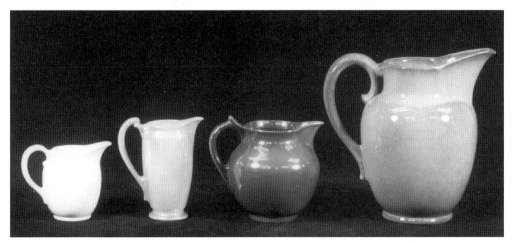

Cowan Pottery made everyday items that were both simple and attractive. R. Guy Cowan was a chemist and artist, and he used his chemistry knowledge to produce original glazes for his pottery. (Photograph Courtesy of Rocky River Public Library.)

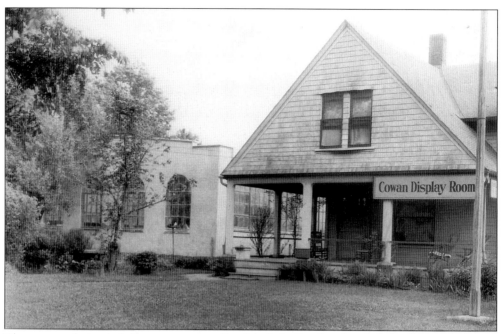

The pottery plant was built on two acres of land on Lake Road and included a display room next to its production facility. There was a large yard in back of the pottery where workers threw out imperfect pieces. Local children would pick through the pile to find pieces that were almost whole to take home to their mothers. (Photograph Courtesy of the Cleveland Press Archives at Cleveland State University.)

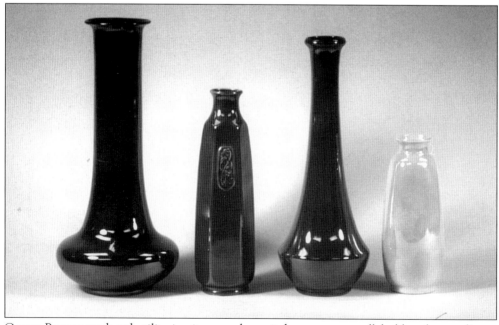

Cowan Pottery produced utilitarian items such as pitchers, vases, candleholders, lamps, dinner services, bookends, nut dishes, and more. Cowan Pottery is highly collectible today. (Photograph Courtesy of Rocky River Public Library.)

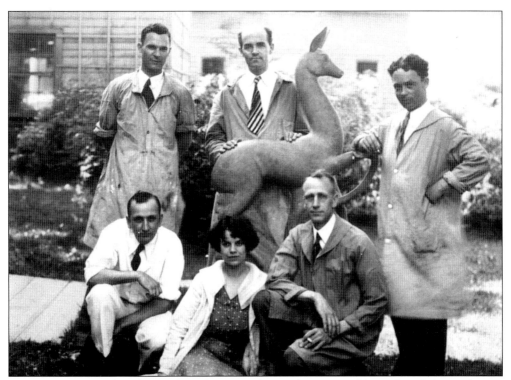

R. Guy Cowan employed a number of artists in his studio. Pictured here, from left to right, are the following: (front row) Waylande Gregory, Thelma Frazier Winter, and R. Guy Cowan;(back row) Paul Bogatay, Jose Martin, and Raoul Jossett. (Photograph Courtesy of Rocky River Public Library.)

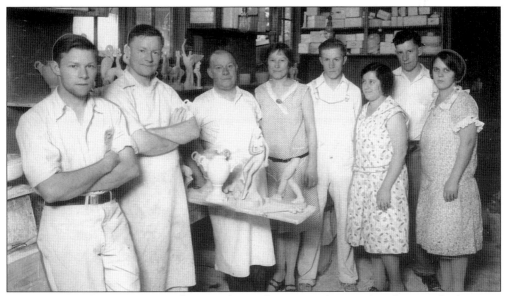

Cowan Pottery had over 40 employees. The production workers in the photograph above are all members of one family—the Brunt family. (Photograph Courtesy of the Cleveland Press Archives at Cleveland State University.)

In the late 1920s, Cowan Pottery was sold in over 1,200 outlets nationwide. Centerpieces consisting of vases, candles, and flower frogs were popular items.

R. Guy Cowan designed the Adam and Eve figurines, which were exhibited in several museums. The figures below are 13 1/2 inches high. (Photograph Courtesy of Rocky River Public Library.)

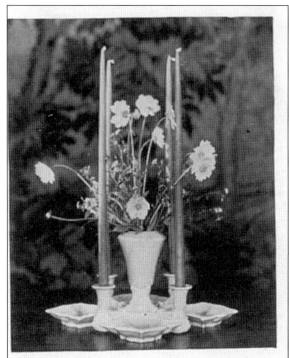

For the Modern Hostess

The newest creation in dinner table ensembles

THE PRINCESS, a new ensemble candelabra, vase and comport set in rare and distinctive pottery from the artist hands of R. Guy Cowan himself.

Compact beyond belief, so that it graces without crowding the smallest table, yet sufficiently lovely to transform the most elaborate Sheraton board. This delightful set is obtainable either complete in April Green or in an intriguing combination with four-candle candelabra and detachable vase in the newest Gunmetal Black and Comports (for nuts, candies or hors d'oevres) in Daffodil Yellow, Apple-Blossom Pink or April Green.

Ensemble, complete, $12.00

The Cowan dealer in your community can supply you and show you many other lovely pieces. Or we will ship C. O. D. parcel post, or you may send check with order.

Cowan Potters, Inc., Rocky River, Ohio

COWAN POTTERY

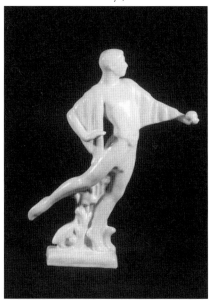

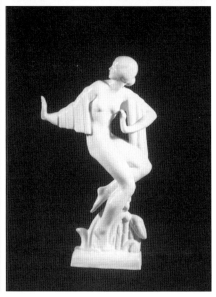

Five

BRIDGES O'ER THE ROCKY RIVER

Before 1821, the only way to cross the river was by ferry. Since Detroit Road was the main highway across northern Ohio, it was important for a bridge on Detroit to be built to help the area grow. The first bridge between Rocky River and Lakewood was built when the township officers organized the construction of a bridge in 1821. They put the following announcement in the Cleveland Newspaper Digest: *"Proposals will be received until the first day of November, by the subscribers, for building a good and substantial bridge across Rocky River, opposite the village of Granger. Chester Dean, Datus Kelley, Trustees of Rockport township."*

All residents of the township were asked to contribute money or labor towards the project. The village of Granger mentioned in the announcement referred to the planned town of Gideon Granger, which never became an official town. Rufus Wright, the tavern owner, paid half of the expenses of the new bridge. He also hosted a party to celebrate the completion of the bridge. According to Crisfield Johnson's History of Cuyahoga County, *"the whisky jug passed merrily around" at the celebration, and Wright himself danced on the tables. The bridge was built slightly above the water, with muddy roads leading down to it on either side.*

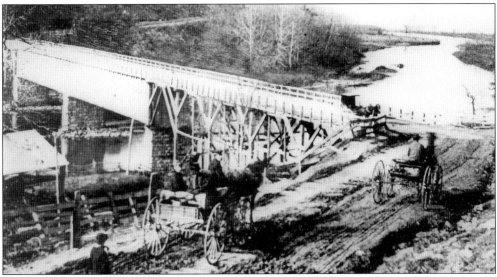

This wooden toll bridge was the second bridge to span the Rocky River. It was built by the Rockport Plank Road Company in the 1850s and started about half way down the side of the hill. It stood just north of the site of the present Detroit Road Bridge. This photograph, circa 1860, was taken from the Lakewood side of the river. At this time Detroit Road was a plank road, a great improvement over the dirt roads of earlier days. (Photograph Courtesy of the Cleveland Press Archives at Cleveland State University.)

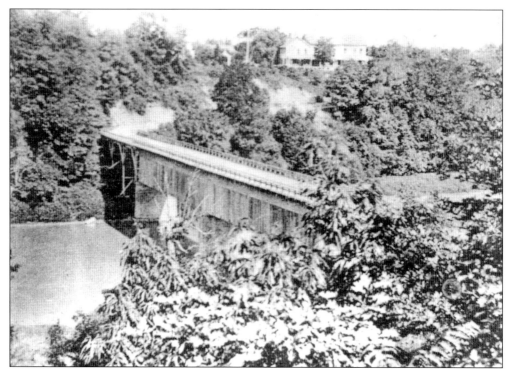

This is another view of the toll bridge, again from the Lakewood side, probably taken years later, as the trees appear to have grown up around the roads leading to the bridge. Farmers' wagons, with their iron-rimmed wheels, made a lot of noise when crossing over the plank bridge. (Photograph Courtesy of Dugan's Barbershop.)

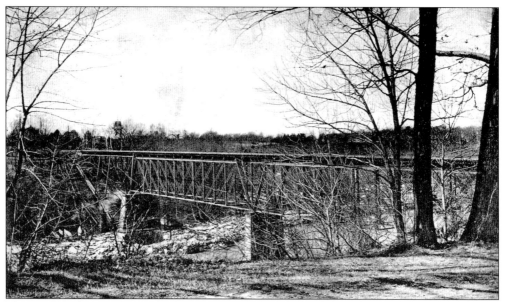

The Nickel Plate Bridge was built in 1882, not long after the Nickel Plate Railroad Company was formed. That same year the Nickel Plate's Buffalo to Chicago run, a distance of 520 miles, was begun.

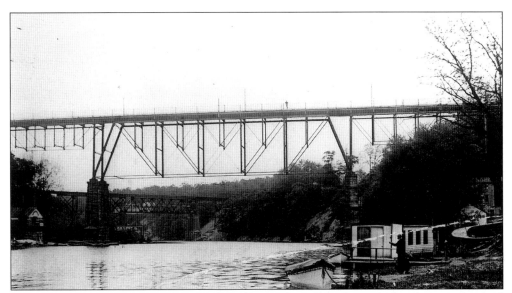

In 1890, an iron bridge was built to replace the wooden toll bridge and, thus, became the third bridge to cross the Rocky River at Detroit Road. This bridge was built at the level of Detroit Road on either side of the river, earning it the nickname "The High Bridge." This was a major improvement over the toll bridge, as it did away with the fairly steep, muddy roads that led down to that bridge. (Photograph Courtesy of Cleveland State University Special Collections.)

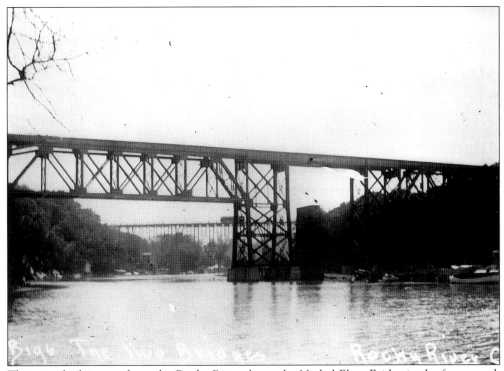

This view looking south up the Rocky River shows the Nickel Plate Bridge in the foreground. An interurban electric streetcar is passing over the iron bridge in the background. (Photograph Courtesy of Cleveland State University Special Collections.)

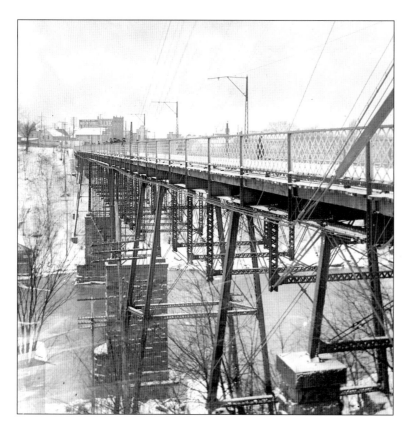

The Iron Bridge, or 1890 Bridge, was also called the "Viaduct." This view of the Viaduct was taken from the eastern end of the bridge looking west into Rocky River. The bridge was 28 feet wide with room for only one set of streetcar tracks. Guardian Bank is the tall building on the other side of the bridge. (Photograph Courtesy of CYC.)

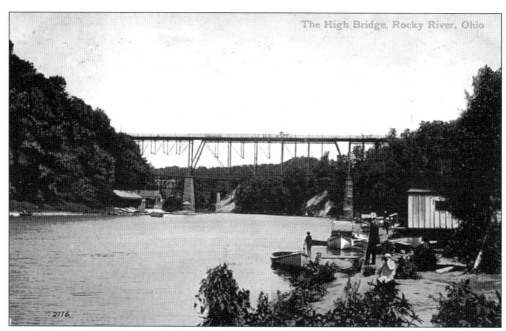

This old postcard of the iron bridge shows boaters on the Lakewood side of the river, which is now part of the Cleveland Metropolitan Park.

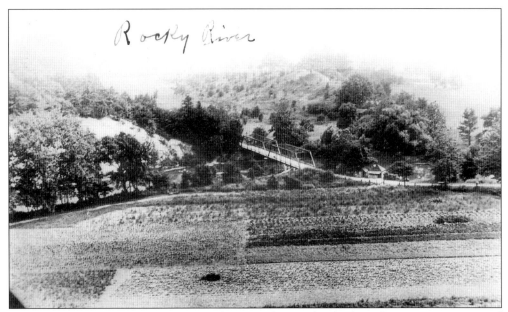

Farther south, up the Rocky River, was the Stranahan Bridge, built in the 1890s. It was named after the family that owned the property down in the valley where the Little Met Golf Course is today. This bridge was part of Old Lorain Road. Today, Fairview Hospital is at the top of the hill in the left of this photograph. This area was part of the original Rockport Township. The first high Lorain Bridge was built in the 1890s. (Photograph Courtesy of the Cleveland Press Archives at Cleveland State University.)

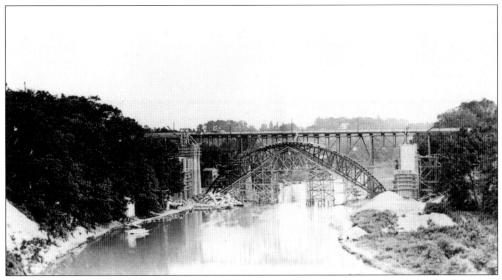

By 1908, the High Bridge was considered dangerous. Construction on a new bridge began in October of the same year. The old bridge, just to the north of the new bridge site, continued to operate until its replacement was completed in 1910.

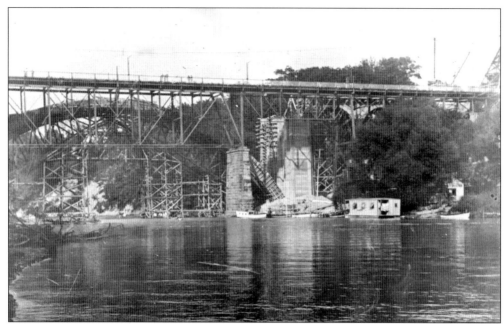

County Engineer Alfred M. Felgate designed the new concrete bridge. The bridge had five approach arches to the main arch—three on the west side and two on the east side. Above, the three small approach arches on the west end are just visible to the right of the main arch. (Photograph Courtesy of Lakewood Historical Society.)

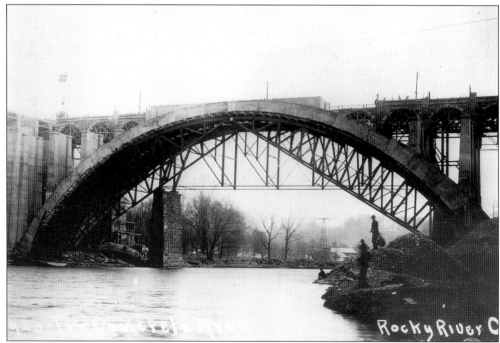

The central arch, which spanned the river, was 280 feet long, making it the longest concrete arch in the world at that time. (Photograph Courtesy of Cleveland State University Special Collections.)

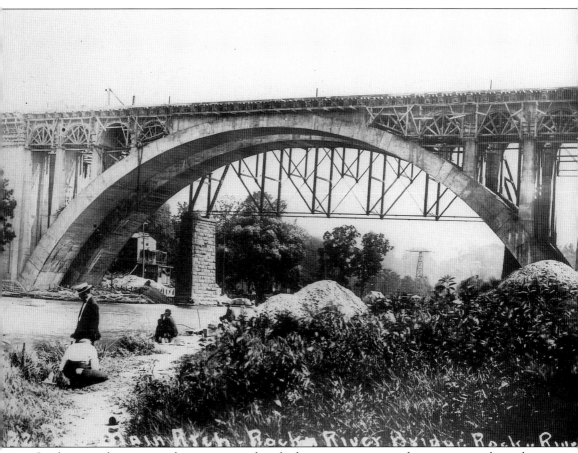

Steel was used to support the concrete arch only during construction; the concrete in the arch itself was not reinforced at all. The floor of the bridge was laid on steel I-beams and was paved with brick. (Photograph Courtesy of Cleveland State University Special Collections.)

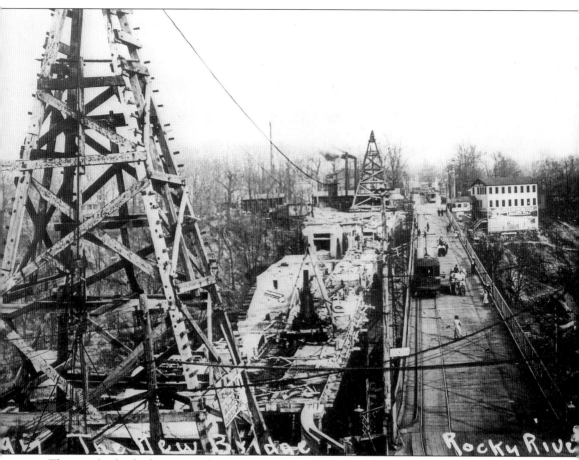

The new bridge had two sets of streetcar tracks in contrast with the previous bridge's one. The temporary towers on either end of the new bridge seen above supported a cableway to transport buckets of concrete. (Photograph Courtesy of Cleveland State University Special Collections.)

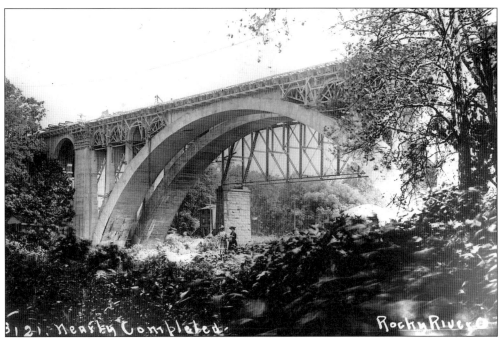

The roadway of the new bridge was 40 feet wide with 8-foot sidewalks on either side. There were four 12-foot-wide observation platforms at the main arch piers. (Photograph Courtesy of Cleveland State University Special Collections.)

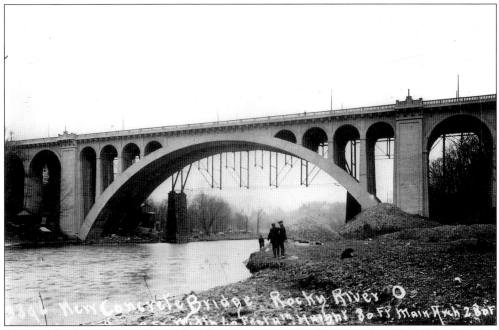

The iron bridge was torn down after the new concrete bridge opened in 1910. The Board of County Commissioners had condemned it in 1908, shortly before the concrete bridge was begun. (Photograph Courtesy of Cleveland State University Special Collections.)

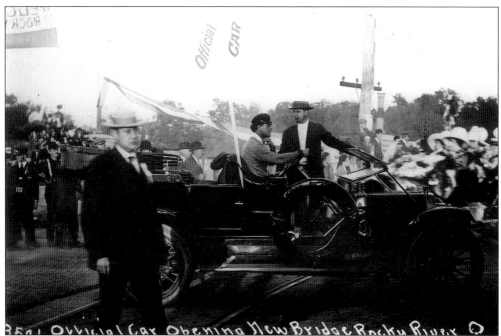

This was the first car to drive over the new bridge on October 10, 1910, when the opening ceremony was held. The bridge opened to regular traffic on October 12, 1910. It was the fourth bridge to cross the river at this location. (Photograph courtesy of Cleveland State University Special Collections.)

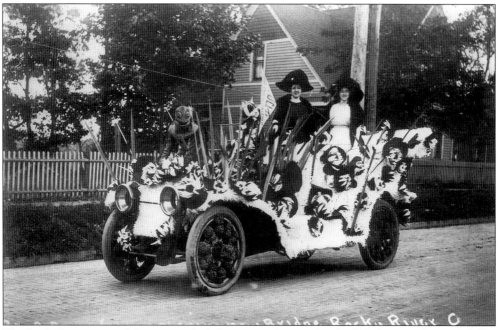

The bridge's opening celebration included music and a parade of 1,500 decorated automobiles, in addition to speeches by various city officials and dignitaries. (Photograph Courtesy of Cleveland State University Special Collections.)

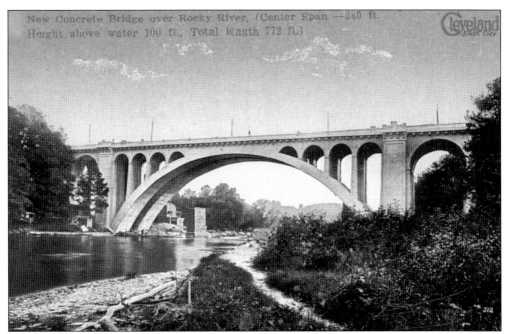

New Concrete Bridge over Rocky River, (Center Span —280 ft. Height above water 100 ft., Total length 772 ft.)

The concrete bridge became known as the Rocky River Bridge. When it opened, it was lauded for its innovative design and beauty. However, within twenty years the bridge became more famous for its traffic jams than its design. Eventually, the bridge began to deteriorate. Despite the fact that it was listed in the National Register of Historic Places, it was demolished in 1980, after a fifth Rocky River Bridge was built. Fortunately for posterity, the three leading arches on the west end of the bridge were saved.

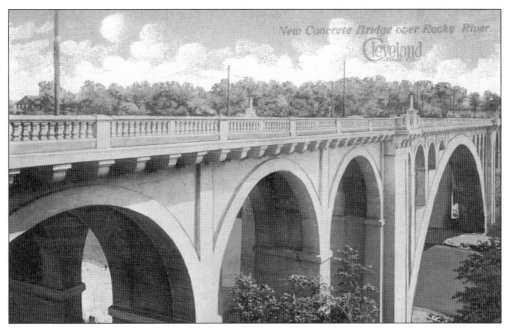

This view of the bridge, looking east, shows the three leading (approach) arches in front of the main arch. These arches appear on the emblem of the city of Rocky River.

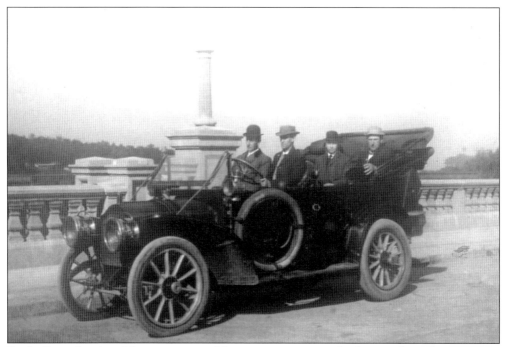

Rocky River developed from a resort and farming town into a suburban residential community, thanks to new modes of transportation, new bridges and improved roads. Early carpoolers, shown above, could easily make the trip into Cleveland for a day's work. (Photograph Courtesy of Lakewood Historical Society.)

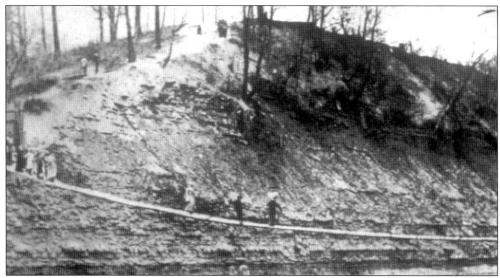

The Grapevine Bridge, as it was called, is seen spanning the Rocky River in this photograph from the early 1900s. The Lakewood end of the bridge was located in the vicinity of Riverside Drive at Hilliard, perhaps on farmland owned by George Mason. Children used the bridge to cross over the river from Lakewood to attend the school on Wooster Road. (Photograph Courtesy of Lakewood Historical Society.)

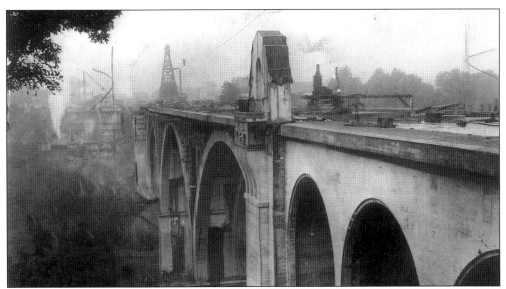

The Hilliard Road Bridge was built in1925 and still stands today. It helped to relieve the traffic congestion on the Rocky River Bridge. Alfred Felgate, the county engineer who designed the Rocky River Bridge, worked on this bridge as well. (Photograph Courtesy of the Cleveland Press Archives at Cleveland State University.)

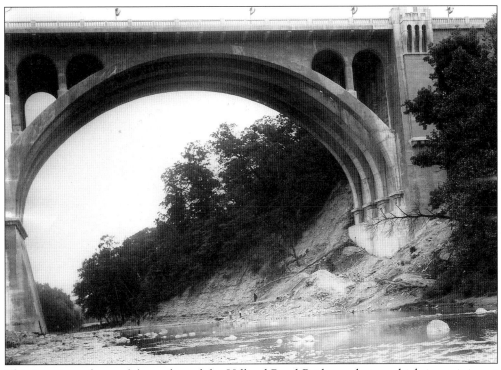

This is a view of one of the arches of the Hilliard Road Bridge, a design which is reminiscent of the Rocky River Bridge. The bridge spans the wide valley and river. The river at this point is rather narrow and, well, rocky. (Photograph Courtesy of the Cleveland Press Archives at Cleveland State University.)

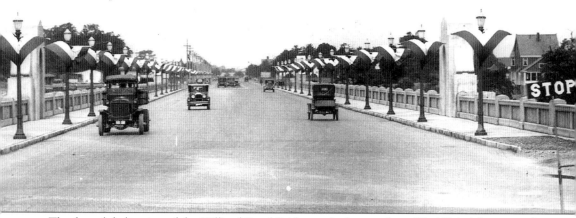

The formal dedication of the Hilliard Road Bridge took place on June 23, 1926. After a parade and speeches, there were fireworks at the west end of the bridge and a carnival and dancing at the east end. (Photograph Courtesy of the Cleveland Press Archives at Cleveland State University.)

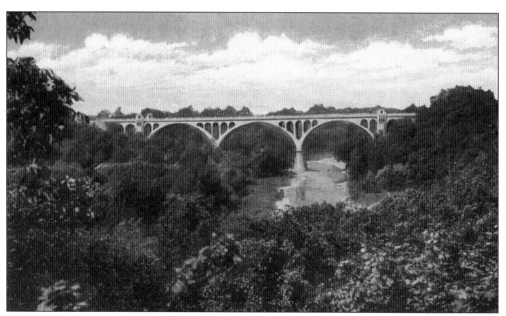

Hilliard Road was named for Richard Hilliard, who at one time owned one-hundred acres in Lakewood, or Rockport as it was known at the time. Hilliard was a businessman and local politician. He was President of the Board of Trustees of the village of Cleveland from 1830 to 1831 and later served as an alderman. He never lived in Lakewood.

Six

POLICE AND FIRE DEPARTMENTS

Local law enforcement first came to Rocky River in 1909, when L. Roy Martin was appointed Marshal. He served in that capacity until 1923, when Matthew Anderson was elected. Anderson was replaced by Gundar Robertson, Jr. in 1927. By the time the village of Rocky River became a city, the head enforcer was known as chief of police. The chief was appointed by the city government; marshals had been directly elected by the residents.

The marshal and his staff were responsible for keeping the general peace. They enforced parking regulations and various village ordinances, such as ones prohibiting the sale of liquor on Sunday and the firing of explosives on the Fourth of July. One important police duty at that time was to direct the traffic over the Rocky River Bridge on Sunday night, when those who had escaped to Rocky River and the West Side for relaxation headed back to Cleveland for the work week.

The fire department was established in1924, with one lieutenant and one fireman. The department had existed on a volunteer basis since 1911. Clarence Anderson, the lieutenant, was appointed chief of the department in 1925. Two more firemen were added that year, making the total number in the department four: Anderson, Charles Duggan, Ray Urban, and Harley Streelberger.

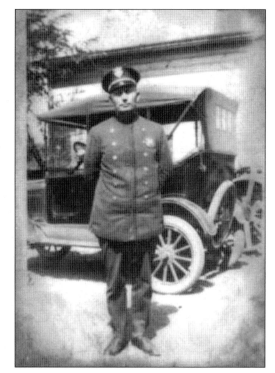

Matthew Andersen was elected marshal in 1923. Records are not clear about whether or not the position of marshal changed to chief of police during his tenure. We know that his replacement, Gundar Robertson Jr., became the first police chief of the city of Rocky River in 1932, when the newly incorporated city reorganized all its departments. (Photograph Courtesy of Rocky River Police Department.)

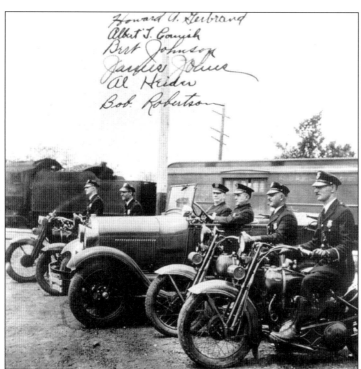

Motorcycles were the first official police vehicles. It wasn't until 1931 that the police department acquired a car. Officers in this 1931 photograph, taken near the train depot, are from left to right Howard A. Gerbrand, Albert J. Cornish, Burt Johnson, James Johns, Al Heider, and Bob Robertson, or Gundar Robertson Jr. as he was officially known. (Photograph Courtesy of Rocky River Police Department.)

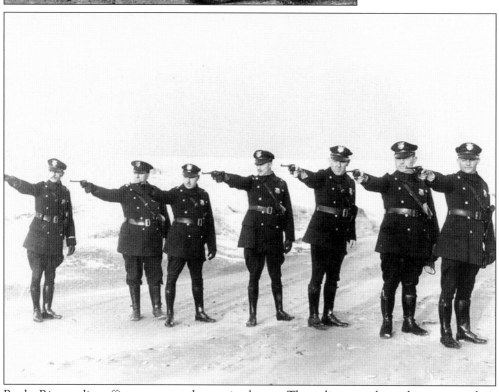

Rocky River police officers competed on a pistol team. The policemen above demonstrate their prowess for the photographer. (Photograph Courtesy of Rocky River Police Department.)

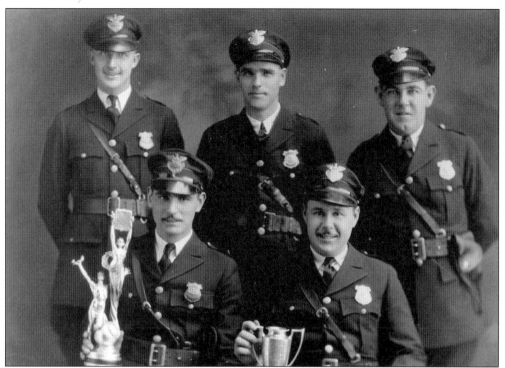

Above is the Ohio championship pistol team of 1935. The Rocky River police officers are pictured, from left to right, as follows: (front row) Bob Robertson and Walter Von Hasse; (back row) Albert Cornish, Al Heider, and Bob Kelley. (Photograph Courtesy of Rocky River Police Department.)

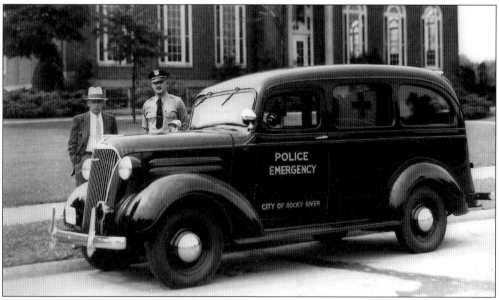

Safety Director L.D. Andrus (left) and Chief of Police Albert J. Cornish pose in front of the library with the city's newest police vehicle in this 1937 photograph. Andrus later became mayor of Rocky River in 1942. (Photograph Courtesy of the Cleveland Press Archives at Cleveland State University.)

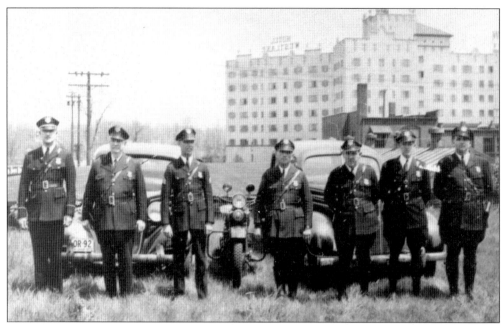

Here, seven of Rocky River's finest pose with vehicles in 1937. The Westlake Hotel looms in the background. The officers, from left to right, are Chief Cornish, Ptl. Johns, Sgt. Woods, Ptl. Johnson, Ptl. Kelley, Ptl. Peterson, and Ptl. Cormier. (Photograph Courtesy of Rocky River Police Department.)

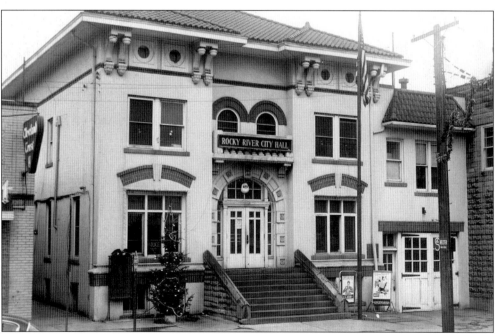

The old city hall on Old Detroit Road was home to the police department for many years until a new city hall complex was built in 1956 on the corner of Hilliard and Wagar. The old city hall building still stands today, sporting a brick facade. (Photograph Courtesy of St. Christopher's Catholic Church.)

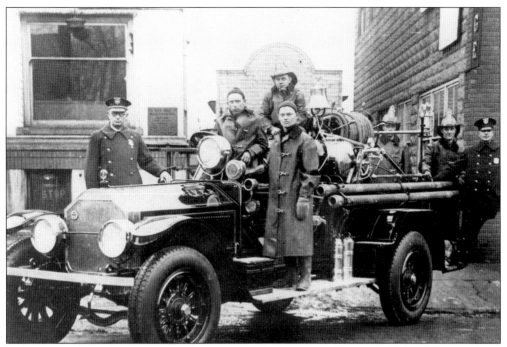

Rocky River firemen pose with their pumper, which was purchased in 1925. The station was located behind the city hall. (Photograph Courtesy of Rocky River Public Library.)

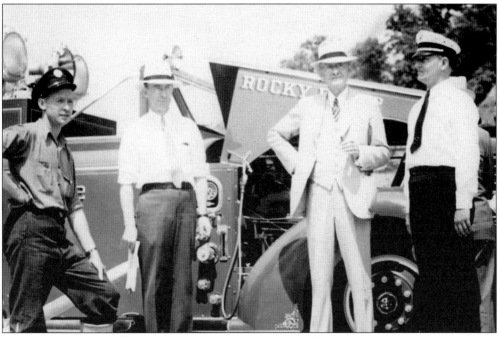

An Inspection Bureau Engineer checks out the new Rocky River fire truck in this photo taken on June 16, 1939. Pictured, from left to right, are Fireman Frank Blanchard, Inspection Bureau Manager H. J. Manning, Mayor Carl Stein, and Fire Chief Clarence Anderson. (Photograph Courtesy of Rocky River Police Department.)

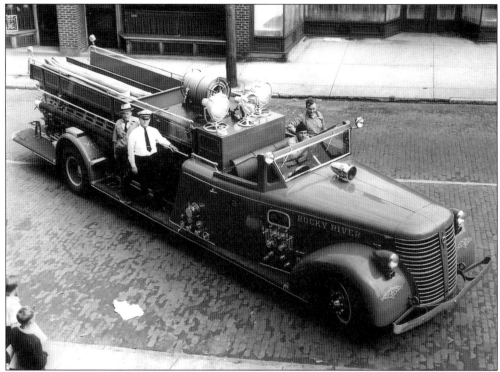

Rocky River purchased this American LaFrance pumper truck in 1939. Showing off the new vehicle, from left to right, are Captain Charles Duggan, Chief Clarence Anderson, Fireman William Sickman (at the wheel), and Fireman Russell Beck. (Photograph Courtesy of the Cleveland Press Archives at Cleveland State University.)

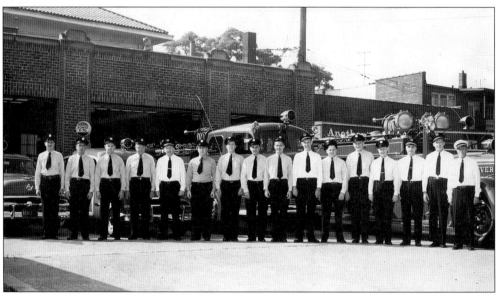

This photograph highlights the firemen and equipment of the 1951 Rocky River Fire Department. The old city hall building can be seen behind the garage. (Photograph Courtesy of Rocky River Police Department.)

Seven
RAILS IN RIVER

The Nickel Plate Railroad was formed in 1881 under the name New York, Chicago & St. Louis Railroad Company. The company started work on its Buffalo to Cleveland to Chicago line that same year. In Lakewood, the company was able to take over the Rocky River Railroad tracks that had been used for the Dummy Railroad. A railroad bridge over the Rocky River was completed in 1882, and railroad service through Rocky River was underway. The Nickel Plate Railroad tracks are the same tracks that run through the city today. The rail companies controlling the tracks have changed over time, as have the rail services, but the tracks have not moved.

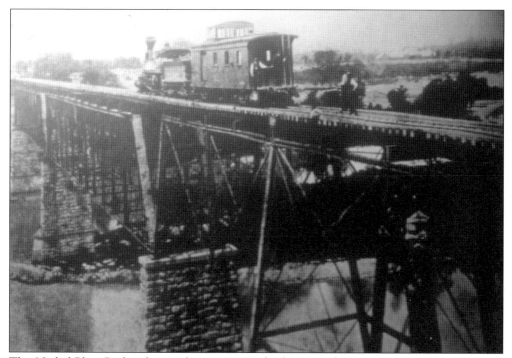

This Nickel Plate Railroad steam locomotive and caboose made a test run over the new Nickel Plate Railroad Bridge in 1882. That same year, trains were running through Cleveland between Buffalo and Chicago.

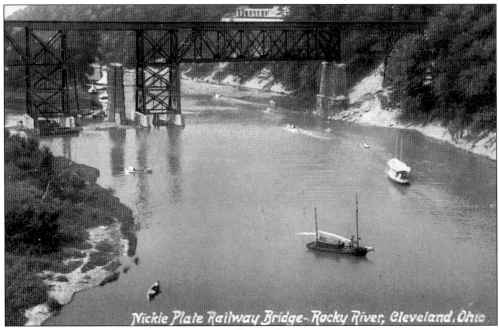

This postcard from the early 20th century shows pleasure boats on the Rocky River on the south side of the Nickel Plate Railroad Bridge. Fishing was very good on the river. Among the fish caught in those days were sturgeon.

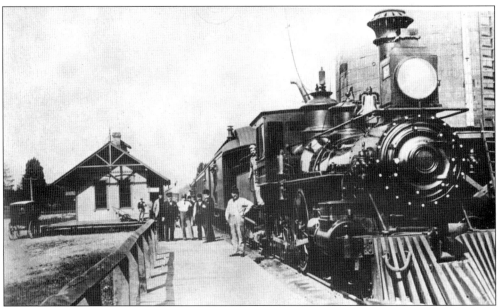

The train depot for the Nickel Plate Railroad was built in 1882. It still stands today, at the bottom of West 192nd Street, which is also known as Depot Street. Rocky River probably got a depot in town thanks to Daniel P. Eells, a resident of Rocky River and one of the major investors in the new railroad. (Photograph Courtesy of Rocky River Public Library.)

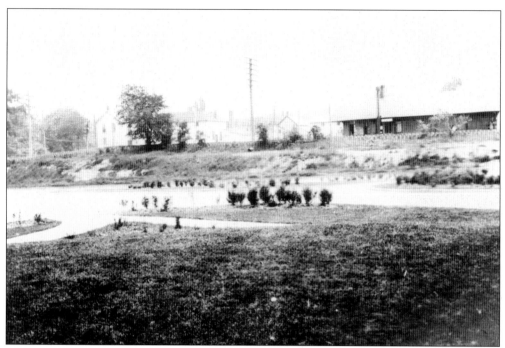

This is a view of the north side of the depot taken from the Lake Road area. The depot is one of the oldest buildings in Rocky River.

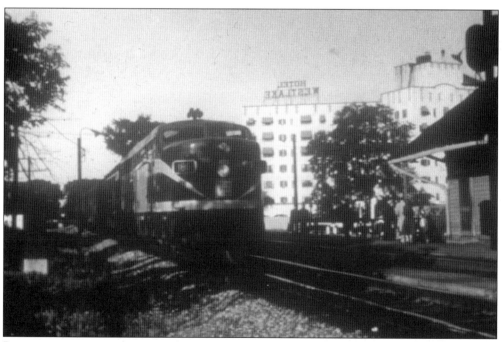

Passenger service to Chicago and New York was available on the train for many years. It was also possible to use the train to commute to Cleveland. Freight deliveries to Rocky River included large shipments of coal for the greenhouses. (Photograph Courtesy of Lakewood Historical Society.)

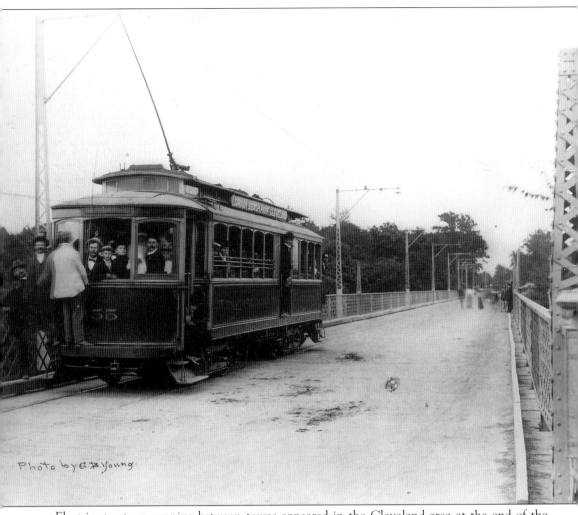

Photo by E. B. Young.

Electric streetcars running between towns appeared in the Cleveland area at the end of the 19th century. Known as interurbans, these streetcar lines offered an alternative to the steam railway or the horse and cart. A number of different lines existed in the Cleveland area, including the Lorain & Cleveland line, which started service in 1897. Once the cars reached Rocky River via the 1890 bridge, they traveled on tracks that ran parallel to and a quarter mile to the south of Lake Road. Above, a Lorain & Cleveland car crosses the High Bridge over the Rocky River in 1898. (Photograph Courtesy of Cleveland State University Special Collections.)

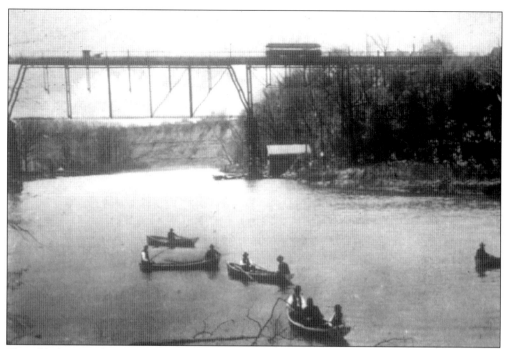

This old photograph from the late 1890s shows an interurban car crossing the High Bridge. A horse and buggy can be seen on the left side of the bridge. The Rocky River was a very popular and productive place to fish at that time. (Photograph Courtesy of Lakewood Historical Society.)

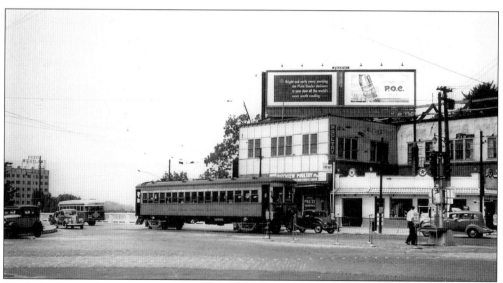

The Lake Shore Electric was an interurban electric railway that operated from 1901 until 1938. The LSE consisted of a number of older lines, including the Lorain & Cleveland. It offered service from Cleveland to Toledo, with local service to points in between. Tickets for the LSE could be purchased at Coulter's Drug Store, on the east end of the Rocky River Bridge in Lakewood. Above, an LSE westbound car prepares to cross the bridge in this 1930s photo. Coulter's stood to the right of the gas station, just outside of the frame of this photograph. (Photograph Courtesy of Cleveland State University Special Collections.)

THE LAKE SHORE ELECTRIC RAILWAY

FAST LIMITED AND LOCAL SERVICE

Leaving Interurban Station at Coulter Drug Store

ROCKY RIVER

TO POINTS WEST AS FOLLOWS:

Beach Park	Clyde	Genoa	Lorain	Sandusky
Bellevue	Detroit	Gibsonburg	Monroeville	Toledo
Berlin Heights	Elyria	Huron	Norwalk	Vermilion
Castalia	Fremont	Lima	Ruggles	Woodville

SCHEDULE OF TRAINS — EASTERN STANDARD TIME

IN EFFECT AUGUST 11, 1930

LIMITED and EXPRESS TRAINS

* 6:02 a. m.	Express to Toledo-Detroit
* 8:02 a. m.	Limited to Toledo
**10:02 a. m.	Express to Toledo-Detroit
*12:02 p. m.	Limited to Toledo
** 2:02 p. m.	Express to Toledo-Detroit
* 4:02 p. m.	Limited to Toledo
** 6:02 p. m.	Express to Toledo-Detroit
* 8:02 p. m.	Express to Toledo
9:02 p. m.	Local to Sandusky
12:00 m.	Local to Sandusky

*Via Sandusky—Making direct connection at Ceylon Junction for Berlin Heights, Norwalk, Monroeville, Bellevue and Clyde.

**Via Norwalk—Making direct connection at Ceylon Junction for Huron, Sandusky and Castalia.

Connections at Toledo with the "Short-Way-Lines" for Adrian, Ann Arbor, Jackson and Flint, Michigan.

LOCALS
TO BEACH PARK AND LORAIN

6:32 a. m.	5:02 p. m. (Note)
8:02 a. m.	* 5:37 p. m.
9:32 a. m.	6:32 p. m.
11:02 a. m.	8:02 p. m.
12:32 p. m.	9:02 p. m.
s 1:17 p. m.	10:32 p. m.
2:02 p. m.	12:00 m.
3:32 p. m.	12:30 a. m.
* 4:32 p. m.	

TO BEACH PARK ONLY

* 8:32 a. m.	c 10:32 a. m.
* 8:47 a. m.	e 5:17 p. m.
* 8:55 a. m.	* 6:02 p. m.
c 9:15 a. m.	9:32 p. m.
* 10:02 a. m.	

* Daily except Sundays and Holidays.
e Daily except Saturdays, Sundays and Holidays.
s Saturday only.
c Sundays only.
Note:—To Ceylon Junction Week Days only.

Special Car and Special Party Rates to All Points Upon Application

Ask Agent about Ten Trip Ticket and Parcel Dispatch Service

Detailed Information on All Matters Pertaining to Rates or Trains from

THE LAKE SHORE ELECTRIC RAILWAY

W. D. COULTER, Ticket Agent
ROCKY RIVER, OHIO

The LSE ran roughly parallel to the Lake Erie shoreline from Cleveland to Toledo—a distance of 120 miles. It provided fast, clean transportation from town to town and offered many an opportunity to get away on summer weekends to resorts and amusement parks. The line was very successful in the days before automobiles became affordable, as the only other options for travel were steam railroad or horse. (Photograph Courtesy of Cleveland State University Special Collections.)

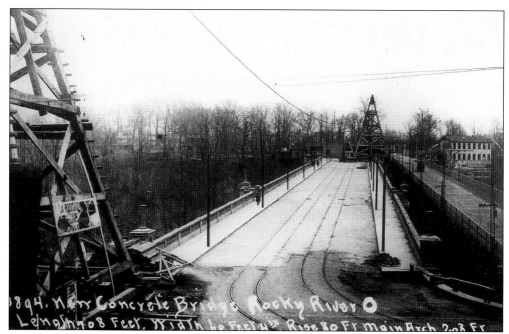

1894. New Concrete Bridge Rocky River O
Length 708 Feet. Width 60 Feet. Rise 80 Ft Main Arch 203 Ft

Initially, the interurbans used the 1890 High Bridge. This bridge had only one track for a streetcar, which limited the interurban car traffic. By 1908, the growing population in the area was causing traffic to increase, and the safety of the bridge was questionable. The new concrete Rocky River Bridge, completed in 1910, had two interurban tracks (as well as plenty of room for cars) and made it possible for the LSE to expand its services. Above, one streetcar track can be seen on the High Bridge at right while the new Rocky River Bridge awaits completion. (Photograph Courtesy of Cleveland State University Special Collections.)

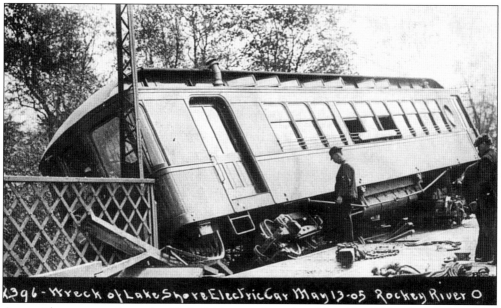

L396 - Wreck of Lake Shore Electric Car May 13-05 Rocky River O

An accident occurred on the High Bridge on Saturday, May 13, 1905, when Lake Shore Electric westbound car number 64 derailed halfway across the bridge.

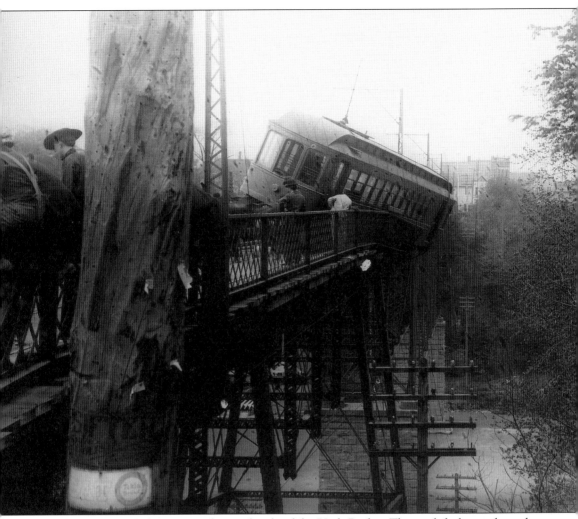

The streetcar tracks were on the north side of the High Bridge. The car left the tracks and ran through the railing of the bridge. It hung off the side, dangling over the river 100 feet below. (Photograph Courtesy of Cleveland State University Special Collections.)

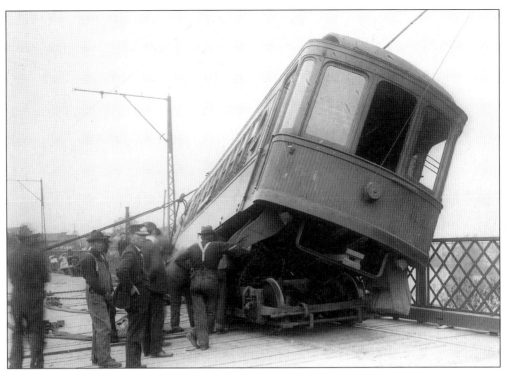

All passengers managed to get out of the car safely. One of them was Warren Bicknell, the president of the LSE. Workers were able to pull the car back onto the bridge. (Photograph Courtesy of Lakewood Historical Society.)

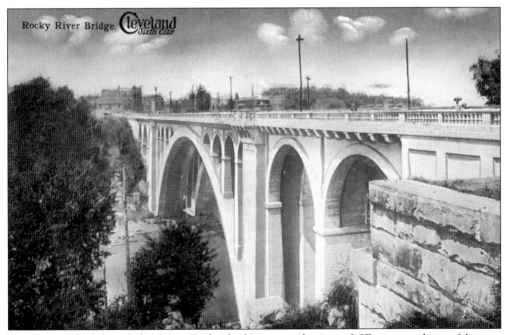

This postcard of the Rocky River Bridge looking west shows an LSE car traveling safely over the sturdy new concrete bridge.

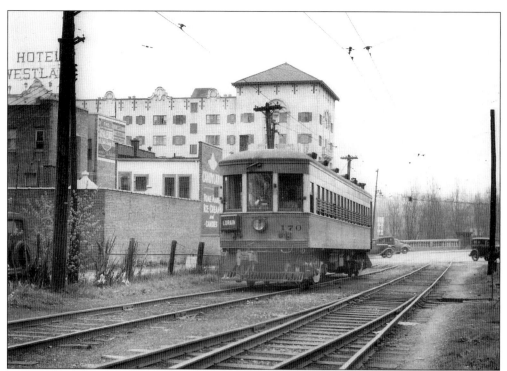

The first stop of the westbound LSE after crossing the Rocky River was on Wooster Road, across from the south end of the Westlake Hotel. This was known as Stop 1. At one point there was a phone at this stop for the conductor to call ahead to the crossing guard on Detroit Road. The photo above shows Car 170 on a local run to Lorain in 1936. (Photograph Courtesy of Cleveland State University Special Collections.)

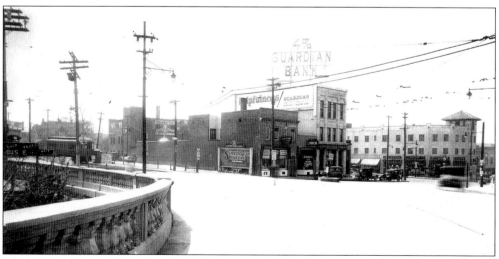

This 1920s photograph is taken from the west end of the Rocky River Bridge looking towards Blount Street. On the left side of the photograph is an LSE car at Stop 1. Candyland is in the center of the picture. At the far right of the photo, the building housing the Sprague Grocery (see page 43) can barely be seen behind the large newer building on the north corner of Old Detroit Road. (Photograph Courtesy of Cleveland State University Special Collections.)

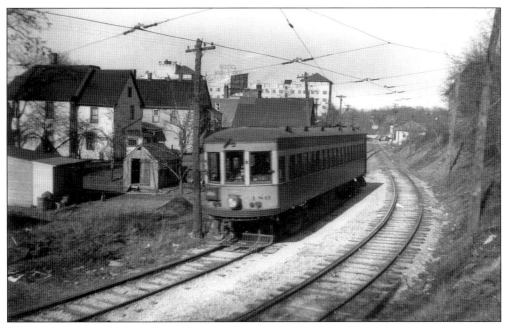

Car 180 above is traveling away from Stop 1, heading west and curving north towards Detroit Road, which was Stop 2. The "new" Detroit Road today roughly follows the line of the LSE tracks. (Photograph Courtesy of Cleveland State University Special Collections.)

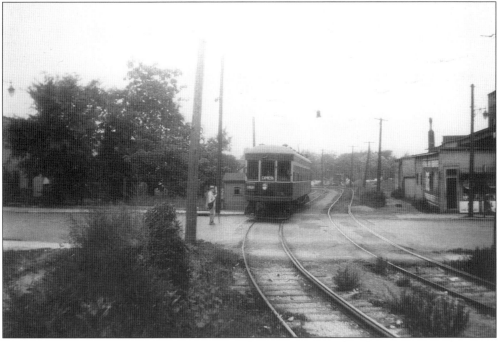

A Cleveland-bound car crosses Detroit Road, where the LSE employed a crossing watchman, in this 1936 photo. The watchman's hut is just left of the tracks. Today, West 192nd street lies where these tracks did. The building on the right served as the Rocky River Post Office in the 1930s. (See page 29.) (Photograph Courtesy of Cleveland State University Special Collections.)

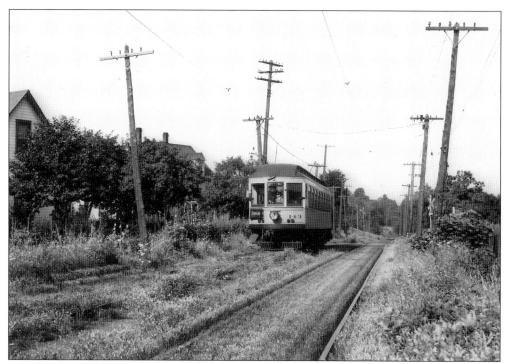

After heading south a few hundred feet along the line of today's West 192nd, the tracks turned westward. The photograph above shows the tracks at the Linda Street crossing, or Stop 3, looking towards the west. (Photograph Courtesy of Cleveland State University Special Collections.)

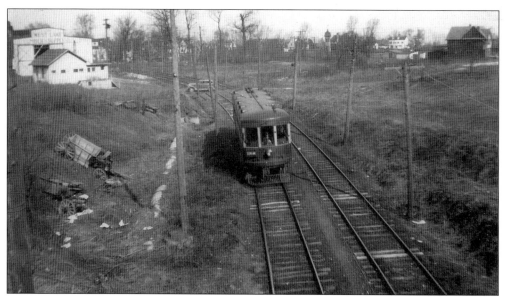

The clock tower at Lake Road and Avalon is visible on the right side of this photo to the left of the white house, which is on Morewood Parkway. The large building on the far right sits on the corner of Kensington Road and Lake Road. The road crossing the tracks no longer exists. According to a 1926 map of Rocky River, this was a secondary road that extended Stratford to Kensington Road. (Photograph Courtesy of Cleveland State University Special Collections.)

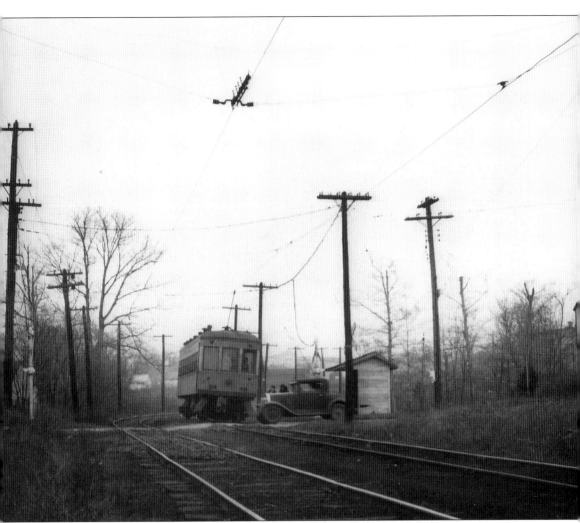

This LSE car has just crossed Morewood Parkway, Stop 4, and is heading east. The tracks in the foreground ran through the island of land that runs down the middle of Beaconsfield Boulevard today. The building at the far right of the photo is part of a house which still stands today. A garage has since been added to its north side. (Photograph Courtesy of Cleveland State University Special Collections.)

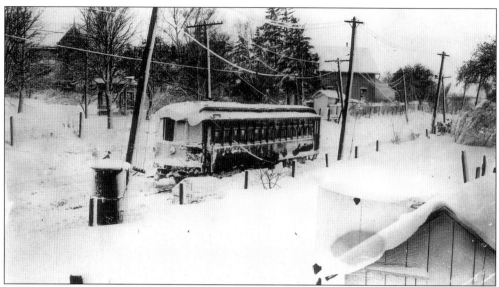

Heavy snow was a challenge for the interurban. Plows and sweepers were attached to special cars to try to clear tracks of ice and snow. Crews would work with snow shovels when needed. The coach above sits stranded somewhere on the tracks in Rocky River due to fallen wires, probably from ice. (Photograph Courtesy of Cleveland State University Special Collections.)

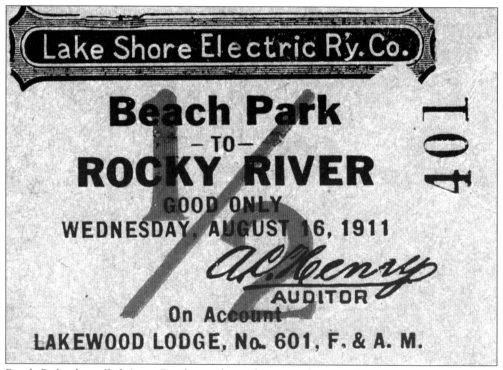

Beach Park, also called Avon Beach, was located seven miles east of Lorain. The LSE owned a power plant there as well as 65 acres of lakefront property. Clevelanders would travel out on the interurban to picnic, to swim, and to visit an amusement park located there. This ticket indicates that a group from the Lakewood Lodge No. 601 had an outing to the beach on August 16, 1911.

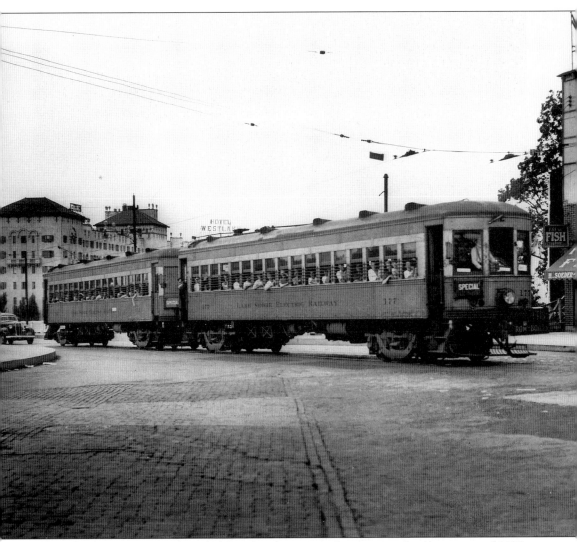

LSE cars could have been chartered for special events and excursions. In the summer of 1937, the Lorain Boys' Club chartered these two cars, shown above just crossing the Rocky River Bridge into Lakewood. Perhaps they were headed to an Indians game downtown. (Photograph Courtesy of Cleveland State University Special Collections.)

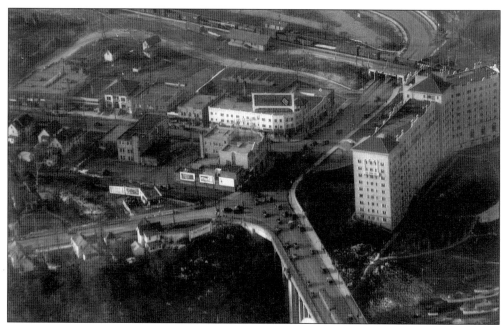

Streetcars cross the Rocky River Bridge in the photograph above, which offers a complete view of the old downtown section of Rocky River in the late 1920s or early 1930s. The tracks for the street car are hard to see, but they turn left off the bridge at about a 120 degree angle, run along behind the businesses and houses on the south side of Detroit Road, and turn right heading towards Detroit just off to the left side of the photograph. After crossing Detroit along the line of West 192nd Street, the tracks turn sharply left and run parallel to the Nickel Plate railroad tracks. (Photograph Courtesy of Cleveland State University Special Collections.)

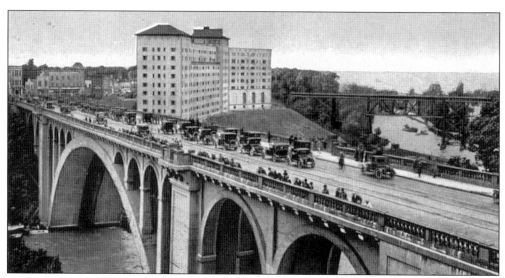

The two empty tracks of the LSE can be seen on the Rocky River Bridge in this postcard. The increasing availability and affordability of automobiles contributed to the demise of the interurban. The Lake Shore Electric Company ceased to operate and exist by 1937. As this postcard illustrates, automobile traffic was quite heavy on the concrete bridge.

Eight
CYC

The island at the mouth of the Rocky River has been the home of the Cleveland Yachting Club, or its predecessors, since 1906. The island was initially considered part of Lakewood, since the west channel was the main channel of the river, dividing the island from the village of Rocky River. After 1918, when the Rocky River Dry Dock Company changed the course of the river, the east channel became the main river channel. The island was annexed to the city of Rocky River in 1946.

As of February 2000, the island had no official name. It has been referred to as Indian Island, since Indians gathered there in the past. Some histories report that Indians buried their dead on the island, which earned it the name Dead Man's Island. Today, many people refer to it as Yacht Club Island. The island became the property of the Cleveland Yachting Club in 1949.

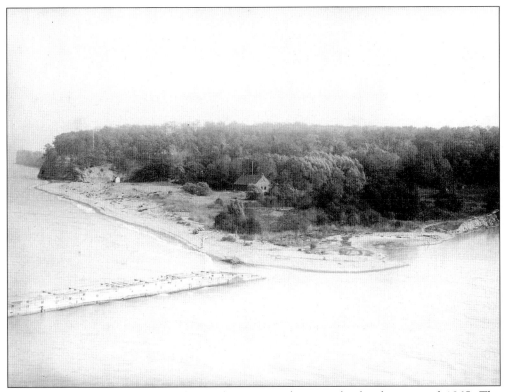

This is a view of the mouth of the Rocky River and eastern bank taken around 1865. The building in the photo is the Rockport Pump House.

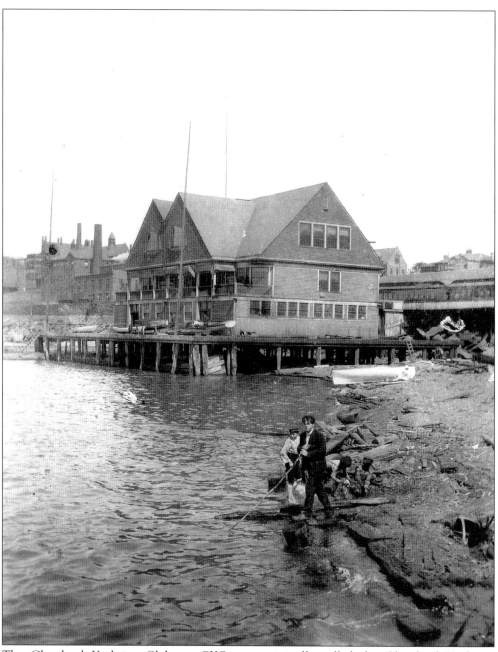

The Cleveland Yachting Club, or CYC, was originally called the Cleveland Yachting Association. It was founded in Cleveland in 1878 by the Hon. George W. Gardner, mayor of Cleveland in 1885–86 and 1889–90. CYA's clubhouse was located at the East Ninth Street Pier. (Photograph Courtesy of the Cleveland Press Archives at Cleveland State University.)

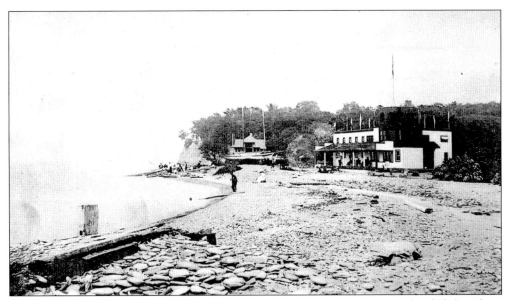

Lakewood Yacht Club was formed in 1899, when A.J. Phelps, boat owner, decided that there should be a yacht club at Rocky River. He got together with other boat owners, and, in March 1900, the LYC held its first meeting. In 1901, the newly formed club signed a ten-year lease for a clubhouse site at the lagoon and beach on the east bank of the Rocky River. In that same year, a small clubhouse was built on Clifton Park Beach. By 1902, members decided that a bigger clubhouse was needed, and a second building was added at the west end of the beach.

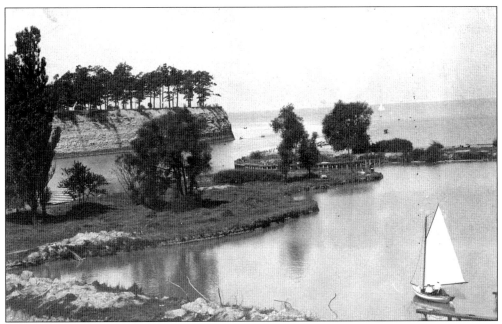

This boat is getting ready to sail out of the lagoon into the lake in the early-20th century photograph above. By 1904, the LYC had 122 members and 54 boats. (Photograph Courtesy of CYC.)

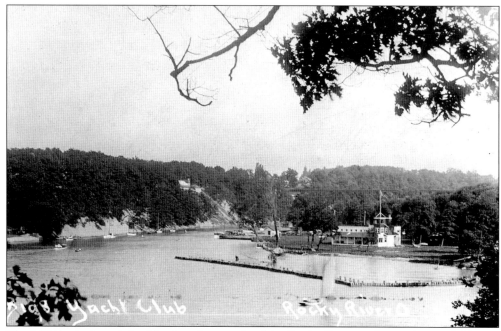

The LYC had selected the island at the mouth of the Rocky River as the site for its clubhouse back in 1901. By 1906, the club was able to purchase the island. The big LYC clubhouse was moved from Clifton Park Beach to the north end of the island on June 1, 1908.

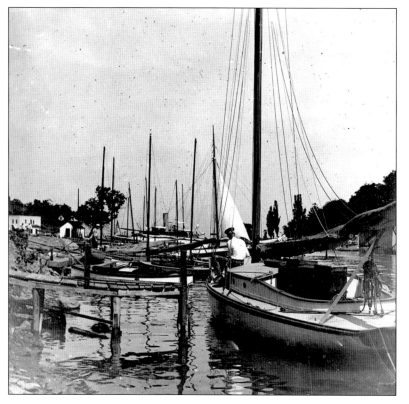

These yachts are moored on the east side of the island. The only way for LYC members to get to the island was by ferry from Clifton Park. The large stones used for the ferry landing at Clifton Park are still there today. (Photograph Courtesy of CYC.)

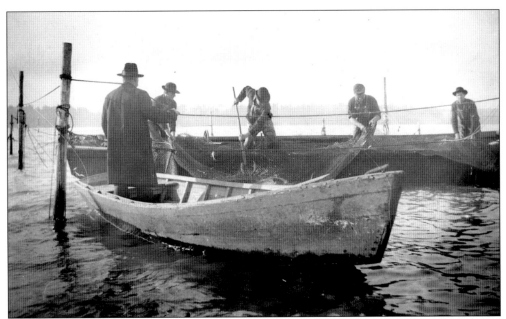

Fishing was a very productive business in the 1900s. George Gerlach, a member of the early CYC, is inspecting his fishing nets in the photograph above. (Photograph Courtesy of CYC.)

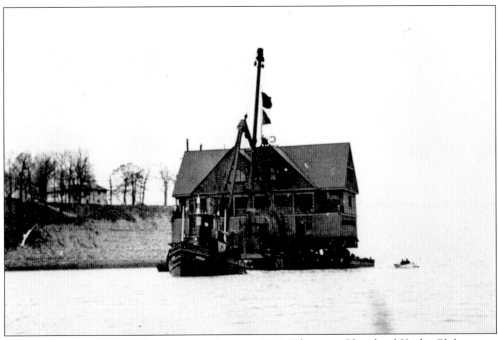

The LYC and CYA agreed to merge in January 1913. The new Cleveland Yacht Club was to have two clubhouses. The clubhouse on East Ninth Street was renovated; however, the downtown clubhouse was not profitable, so the club decided to move the building to the island in Rocky River. The building was loaded onto skids, which were placed on three barges lashed together. On November 29, 1914, the clubhouse made the trip to Rocky River. (Photograph Courtesy of CYC.)

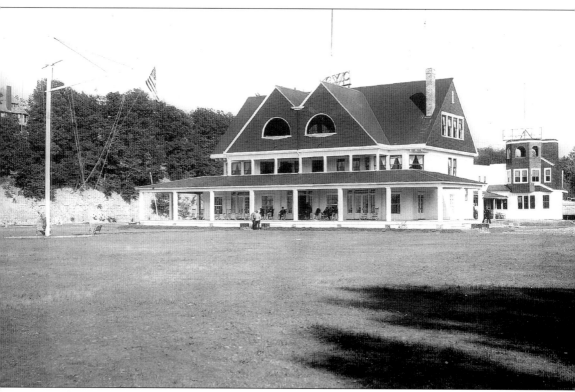

Back on the island, the LYC building was rotated so that it faced west. The Cleveland clubhouse, with the veranda facing the lake, was attached to the original LYC building. A new dining room was added to the new clubhouse. (Photograph Courtesy of the Cleveland Press Archives at Cleveland State University.)

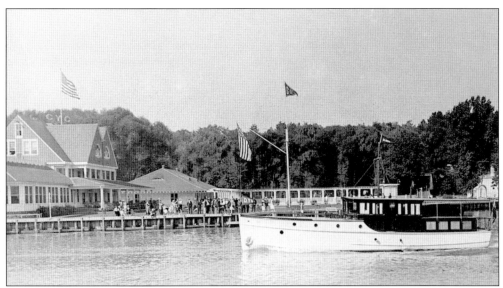

This photograph of the Cleveland clubhouse was taken around 1915, when the CYC was entering its first heyday. By 1918, the membership of the club had grown to 1500. The booming club built a bathing pavilion and recreation room by the river, a dance hall, a swimming pool, and a movie building. Steam yachts, popular at the turn of the century, were slowly being replaced by motor yachts. (Photograph Courtesy of CYC.)

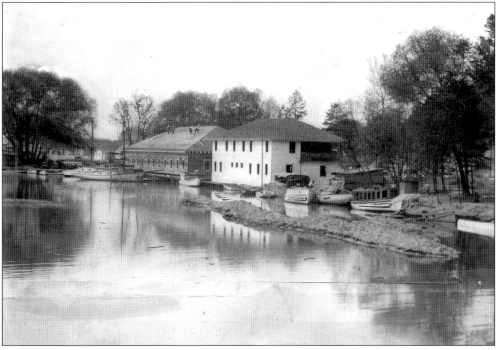

The CYC organized a Summer Naval and Recreation School for Boys during World War I. A mess hall and barracks were built for the school in 1919. The boys slept in tents while the school was in session for six weeks in the summer. Instructors lived in the barracks. (Photograph Courtesy of the Cleveland Press Archives at Cleveland State University.)

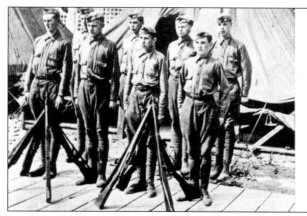

MEMBERSHIP in the C.Y.C. Naval and Recreation School is open to boys, nine to eighteen years of age who are sons of members. Throughout the day, the Cadets are seen in their khaki uniforms with "spiral" rolled puttees and over-seas caps, and in the evening in their navy whites.

Membership in the Naval and Recreation School was open to the sons of CYC members, aged nine to eighteen years. (Photograph Courtesy of CYC.)

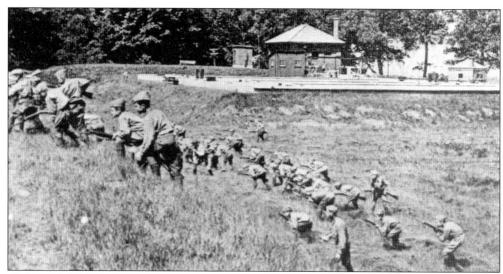

The motto of the School was "Sano in Corpore Mens Sana," or Healthy in Body, Healthy in Mind. The boys, known as cadets, did training exercises and military maneuvers on land and lake. (Photograph Courtesy of CYC.)

Farther down the river, the Rocky River Dry Dock Company was quietly formed in 1917. It was located behind where the Westlake Hotel stands today. Nothing was written about the company at the time, as publicity was unwelcome. The company built four submarine chasers for the French government, our allies during World War I. (Photograph Courtesy of the Cleveland Press Archives at Cleveland State University.)

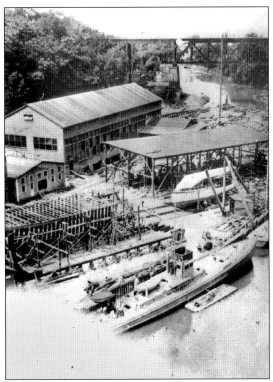

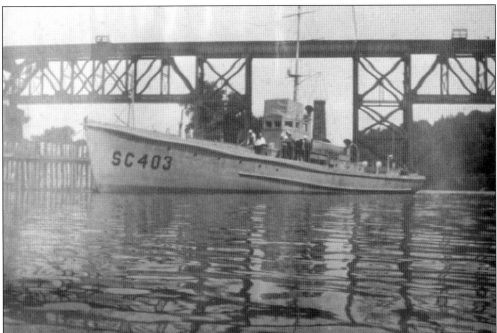

The sub chasers were wooden by design and were made to patrol mine-infested waters in the Atlantic. Wooden boats were less likely to detonate the mines than metal ones, which attracted the magnetized mines. Fifty wooden sub chasers were built in the Great Lakes area during World War I. (Photograph Courtesy of Lakewood Historical Society.)

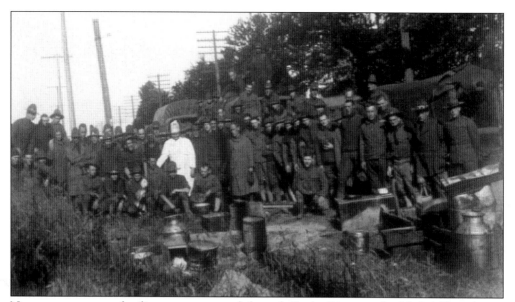

Numerous convoys of military troops passed through Rocky River on the Nickel Plate during World War I. The troops pictured above stopped for lunch somewhere along the tracks in Rocky River. They were on their way to the eastern seaboard and transport ships headed to Europe. (Photograph Courtesy of Lakewood Historical Society.)

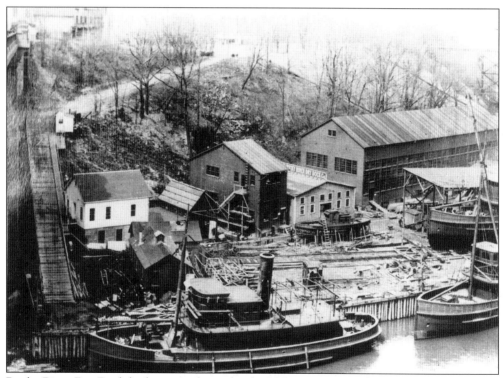

Rocky River Dry Dock built two tugboats for the U.S. government during World War I. The Dry Dock facilities extended into the river and restricted the flow of water in the west channel, allowing silt to build up. (Photograph Courtesy of Rocky River Public Library.)

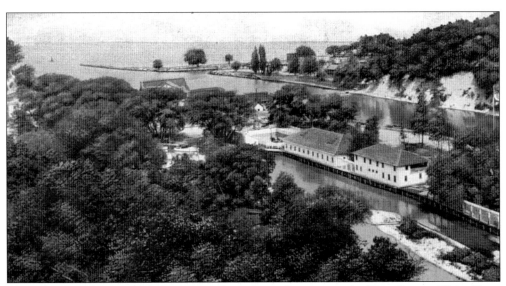

The Cleveland Yacht Club was a popular subject for post cards. The George Klein News Company published the postcard above with the caption: "This view shows one of the pretty spots on Rocky River. Moonlight sailing is a popular and delightful pastime here. Small boats of every description can be seen on the river in summer, which is a wonderful sight. Rocky River empties into Lake Erie."

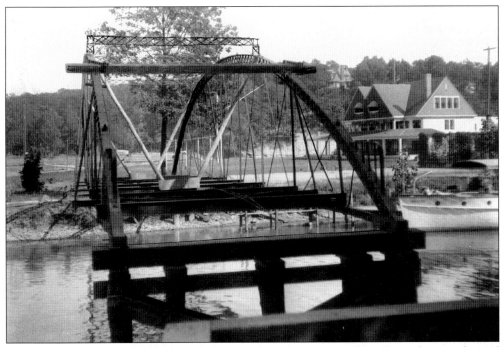

With the Rocky River Dry Dock facilities causing the west channel to silt in, the east channel became the main entrance to the river. The above photograph, taken sometime in the 1920s, shows a permanent bridge constructed over the west channel to connect the island to Rocky River, sometime in the 1920s. (Photograph Courtesy of the Cleveland Press Archives at Cleveland State University.)

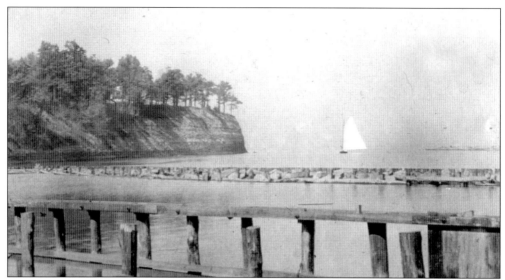

The photograph above, circa 1920, paradoxically shows calm waters but a full sail. After WWI, the CYC fell on hard times and went bankrupt in 1924. Over the course of the next ten years, the club existed under various names, and rented space on the island that it had once owned. In 1934, the newly organized Cleveland Yachting Club began to build up membership. Dues at that time were $10 in contrast with the $500 charged in 1920. (Photograph Courtesy of Lakewood Historical Society.)

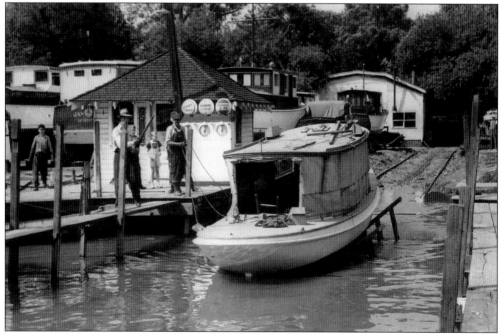

By 1943, when the photograph above was taken, things were running smoothly on the island for CYC. Membership in the club was growing. A group of members purchased the island and formed the Rocky River Island Company, which worked closely with the club to improve the island. The club was able to repurchase the island from the company in 1949. (Photograph Courtesy of the Cleveland Press Archives at Cleveland State University.)

Nine
THE NOT-SO-DISTANT PAST

In 1891, Rocky River became a hamlet. (A hamlet is the smallest form of municipal government, sometimes attached to a larger town.) In 1903, the village of Rocky River was incorporated. That year marks the official beginning of Rocky River as an independent municipality.

In 1930, the town of Rocky River became a city. With both the Detroit Road and Hilliard Bridges connecting Rocky River to points east, the city became a desirable place to live. It was close enough to Cleveland and all its big city attractions, but far enough away to retain an atmosphere of peace and quiet. Rocky River was sometimes referred to as a city of homes.

No city would be complete without local businesses. There are certain businesses in every community that are considered local institutions—businesses that are part of the community's identity. Such places are supported by the citizens not just out of need, but out of loyalty. It is always sad when such businesses cease to exist. However, no business is immune to the changing needs, whims, or tastes of its customers.

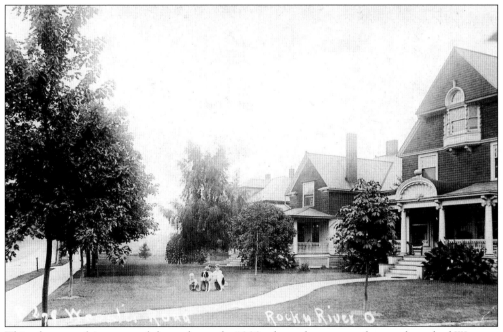

This photographic postcard from the early 1900s shows houses on the north end of Wooster Road, which are still standing today. This road was originally called Mastick Road, after one of the first families who settled in Rocky River.

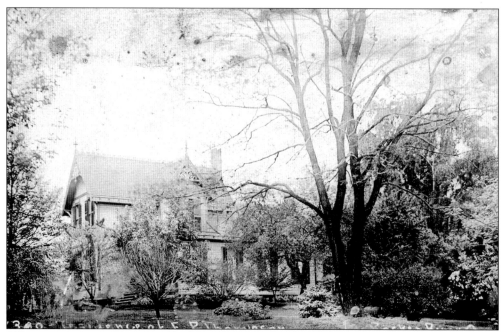

This house belonged to E.P. Thompson. It was on the north end of Wooster Road, like the houses in the previous photograph. Thompson took over the dry goods business and post office from the Geiger & Keyse Company, whose store is pictured on page 25.

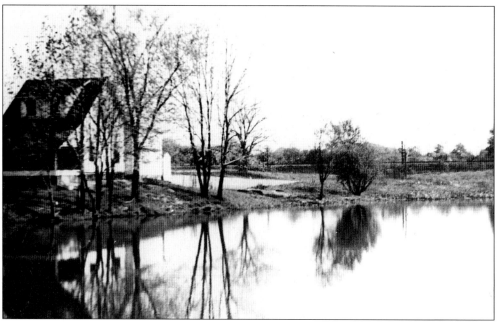

The Bates farm was located between Detroit and Lake Roads in the area where Bates Road is today. The 1874 Rockport Map lists John Bates as the owner of the land. By the 1930s, the Bates family no longer farmed their property. The farmhouse was used as a weekend and vacation home by family members and their friends. (Photograph Courtesy of Rocky River Historical Society.)

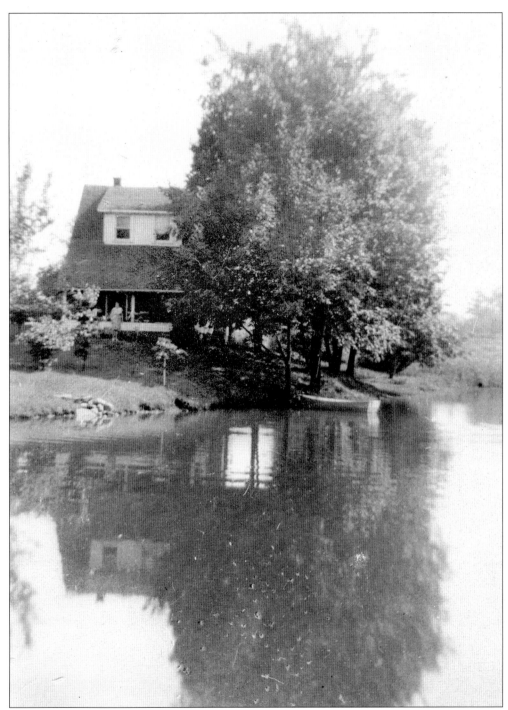

On the porch of the Bates house was a guest book for visitors to sign. Some surprise guests were hobos of the Depression era, who hopped off the trains that ran through the property. They would bathe and fish in the pond. Some of them signed the guest book. The house was torn down in 1962, when less polite uninvited guests—vandals—caused considerable damage to the home and its contents.

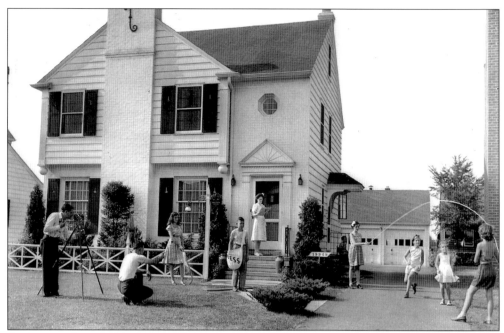

As farms such as the Bates Farm disappeared, neighborhoods began to develop. Although this *Cleveland Press* photograph of the Fred Singer home on Laurel Avenue was staged, it accurately depicts what life was like in the suburbs of the early 1940s. (Photograph Courtesy of the Cleveland Press Archives at Cleveland State University.)

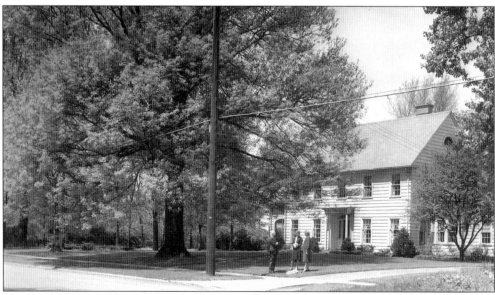

The Beach Cliff neighborhood on the former Clifford Beach property was well-developed by the 1940s. Despite all the building happening around it, the oak tree on the lawn of the Shie house on Avalon was not cut down. The tree was designated a Moses Cleaveland Tree in 1946, the year of the sesquicentennial of the landing of Moses Cleaveland on the Cuyahoga River. Trees given that honor were those that had been around since 1796. Unfortunately, the tree has since been cut down. (Photograph Courtesy of the Cleveland Press Archives at Cleveland State University.)

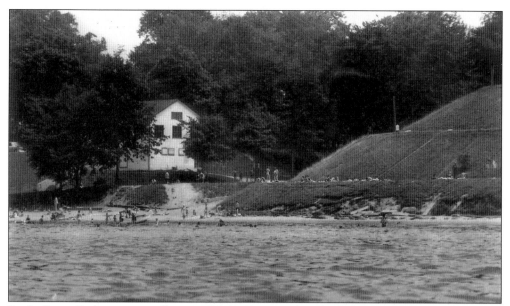

Rocky River Park was originally named Lake Front Park. It had a bathhouse with a concession stand and lifeguard service all summer long. The hill overlooking the park has since eroded, but it was terraced as seen in the photograph above, making it an ideal spot to watch the fireworks on Rocky River Day. That holiday took place in August from the 1930s to the 1970s. It was a day for citizens to celebrate being a part of Rocky River. (Photograph Courtesy of the Cleveland Press Archives at Cleveland State University.)

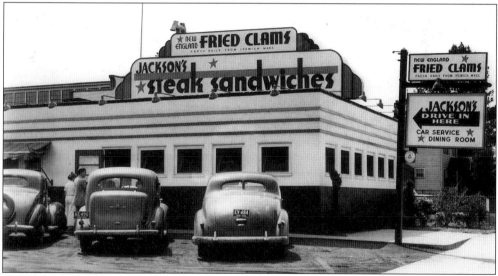

Jackson's Diner opened in 1934 on Lake Road. It offered dining room service as well as car service. The dining room had a model train that ran around the perimeter of the ceiling. After the Jackson's sold the business to the Bearden family in 1948, the diner was re-named Bearden's Restaurant. It was a very popular drive-in in the 1950's, and it stayed open until 2 a.m. on weekends. Over the years the restaurant has been remodeled, but it has always kept its trademark model train. (Photograph Courtesy of the Cleveland Press Archives at Cleveland State University.)

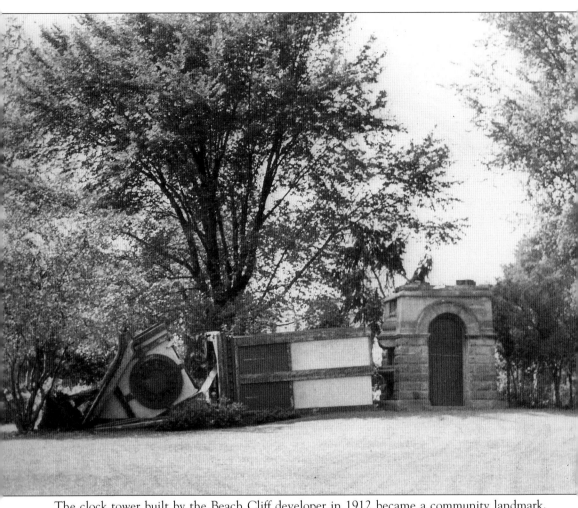

The clock tower built by the Beach Cliff developer in 1912 became a community landmark. The city bought the land around the tower in the 1940s, in order to preserve it. A freak windstorm knocked the tower down on May 12, 1956. The wind did a lot of damage on the west side of Cleveland, especially in Lakewood and Rocky River. The clock tower was re-built exactly like the original around 1990. (Photograph Courtesy of the Cleveland Press Archives at Cleveland State University.)

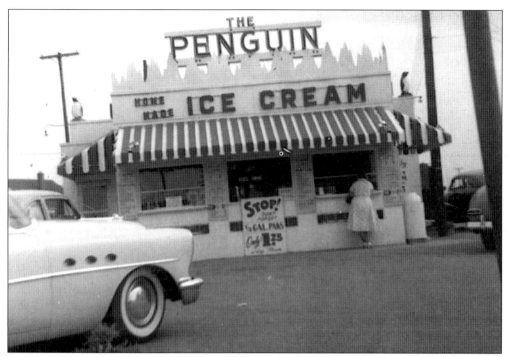

Ewing's Penguin Ice Cream and Frozen Custard Stand stood on the south side of Center Ridge, to the west of Wagar Road. The Ewing family gauged traffic in various parts of Rocky River before deciding on this location. Bob Ewing and his son Bill opened the store after World War II.

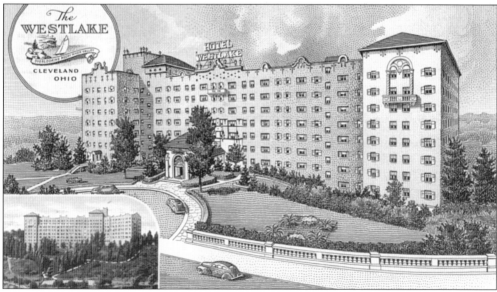

The Westlake Hotel was built on the site of the historic Silverthorn Tavern. It was a hotel where small apartments could be rented for an extended period of time. A 1931 advertisement for the hotel states: "For those that have always wanted suburban living with winter sports at a hotel where comfort and hospitality abound...the Westlake with these unusual features, creates a new style of living at a most moderate rental."

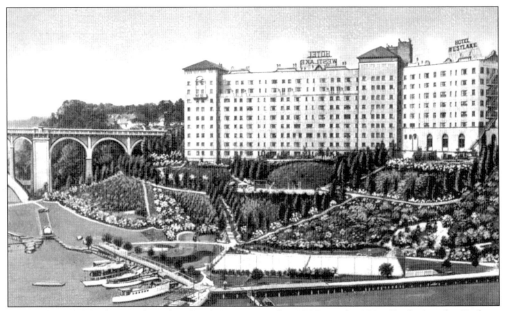

There was no hotel near the Cleveland Airport in the 1920s and 1930s. Both Amelia Earhart and Admiral Richard Byrd stayed overnight at the Westlake when they visited Cleveland. Charles Lindbergh visited the hotel, but did not stay overnight.

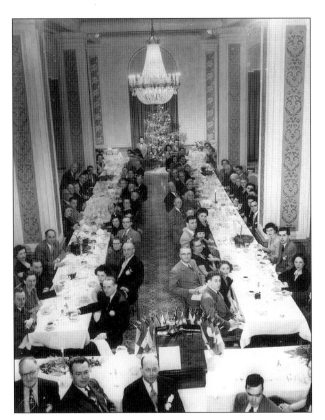

The Westlake Hotel had a restaurant, which was fittingly called the Silverthorn. One level below the restaurant was a beautiful ballroom. The West Shore Lions held a Christmas dinner and party there in 1952. The Silverthorn was closed in 1983, when the hotel was renovated and changed over to condominiums. (Photograph Courtesy of Cleveland Press Archives at Cleveland State University.)

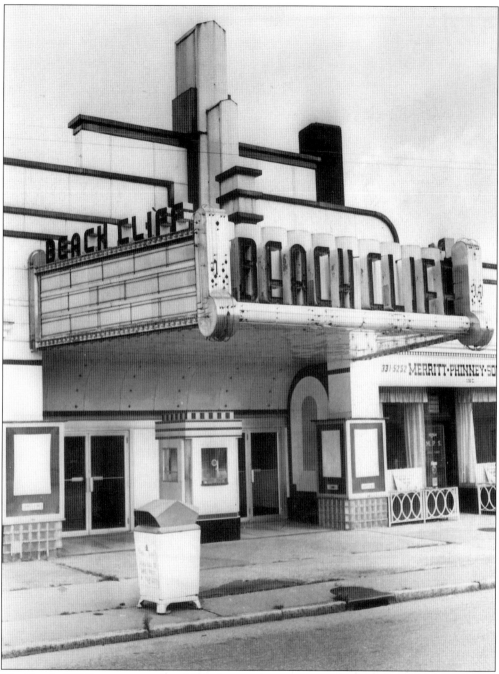

The Beachcliff Theater opened in 1936. It was a big screen movie theater in the old tradition. Like most movie theaters of this type, it closed down when small, multi-screen cinemas appeared. In 1978, it was remodeled into a shopping mall.

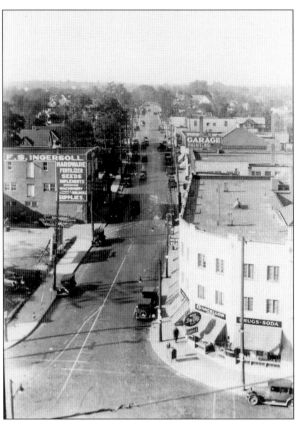

This vista looking west on Detroit Road was taken from one of the upper floors of the Westlake Hotel in the 1920s. The Ingersoll store on the left is the same business seen in photographs of Blount Street in Chapter Two. The business moved to Detroit Road in 1922. Today, Talbot's occupies the old Ingersoll building, while Ingersoll's has moved farther west on Detroit Road. Ingersoll's has been in business since 1906, when F.S. Ingersoll bought the Geiger & Co. hardware business from John Hoag.

This is what Detroit Road looked like in the 1940s, quite different than it does today. Almost all of the businesses shown above are gone and the course of Detroit Road has changed. The Westlake Hotel, although it is only eighty years old, is the successor of the old Wright/Silverthorn Tavern. It has become a new, and very visible, landmark for Rocky River.

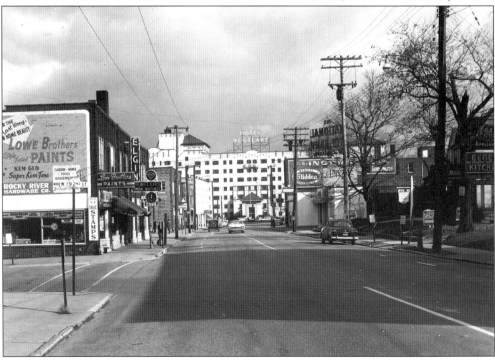

ACKNOWLEDGMENTS

I would like to thank all the institutions that shared their photographs and information with me. The names of these institutions appear under the captions of their photographs.

A big thank you to all the individuals who loaned me their photographs. They are: Janet Bowles Cipriani, Robert J. Fuller, Linda Shie Hickerson, George Jindra, Frieda Schneid Pitts, Ruth Regula, John Schanz, William D. Shie, Ginny Stepler, Jack Sutcliffe, Sally Ewing Turnbull, and Edna and Dick Zeager.

I'd also like to thank Robert Lipkos at Dugan's Barbershop, Maizie Adams at the Lakewood Historical Society, Dick Slaght at the CYC, John Weedon, Victoria Pelz and Julie Mortensen at the Rocky River Public Library, Carol Jacobs at the Rocky River Historical Society, Robin Reinbold at the Rocky River Board of Education, Camron Bussard and Jenny Sehringer for their assistance and support.

Special thanks to my mom and sometimes secretary, Rusty Lestock, for allowing me to take over her home. Thanks to my husband, Macauley Lord, for his encouragement, advice, and editing expertise. Apologies to my dog Moses, who was deprived of all the attention he deserved while I worked on this book. Finally, thank you to Gary Lawless, of Gulf of Maine Books in Brunswick, Maine. When I asked him if Arcadia Publishing had a book about Rocky River, Ohio, he answered: "No. Why don't you write one?"

This book would never have been possible without my uncle, Jack Sutcliffe, who unwittingly sparked my interest in the history of Rocky River by showing me old photographs of the city. This book is dedicated in his memory.

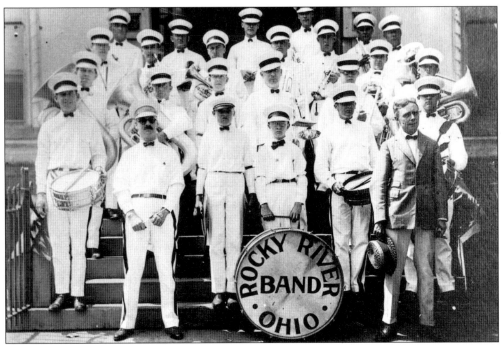

If I could, I would ask the Rocky River Band, circa 1920, to play a song of tribute for everyone who has ever written/photographed/preserved any piece, large or small, of Rocky River history. I am in their debt.

Bibliography

These are the main sources I used. I am especially grateful to Ralph Richards and Ron Gabel, whose history of the city is an excellent source of information.

Bassett, Mark, and Victoria Naumann. *Cowen Pottery and the Cleveland School*. Schiffer Publishing, Ltd.: Atglen, Pennsylvania. c. 1997.

Gabel, Ron, and Ralph D. Richards. *City of Rocky River Golden Jubilee and Ohio Sesqui-Centennial Celebration 1903–1953* or *A History of the City of Rocky River*. The Lakewood Printing Company: Lakewood, Ohio. 1953? (*author's note:* This is a booklet put out for city's Golden Jubilee. Inside it says: "copyright applied for")

Grabowski, John J. and David D. Van Tassel, compilers. *Encyclopedia of Cleveland History*. Accessed at: http://ech.cwru.edu/index.html.

Harwood, Herbert H. Jr. and Robert Korach. *The Lakeshore Electric Railway Story*. Indiana University Press: Bloomington, Indiana. c. 2000.

Johnson, Crisfield, compiler. *History of Cuyahoga County, Ohio Part Third: History of the Townships*. D.W. Ensign & Co. 1879.

Lakewood Files accessed at: http://www.lkwdpl.org/lfiles/

Limited Edition yearbooks of the CYC by various publishers

Rocky River Public Library, vertical files.